KENT HEROES

Brave, Resourceful and True

Bowen Pearse

To Justin and Christina

Other books by Bowen Pearse
Companion to Japanese Britain and Ireland
Kent Women
Sussex Characters

First published in 2002
© Bowen Pearse

Published by JAK and distributed by
Meresborough Books,
7 Oast Park, Spade Lane, Hartlip, Sittingbourne, Kent ME9 7TT
Tel: 01634 388812
Fax: 01634 378501
sales@merebooks.co.uk
www.rainhambookshop.co.uk

Front Cover illustrations - upright: Lady de Mouse of Pembury;
Right from top to bottom: Charles George Gordon in Cairo; Lady Sue
Ryder presented with Benenden School award, by the Princess Royal;
John Baptist Lucian Noel in Tibetan dress.

ISBN 0-9524491-6-7

Designed and Typeset by E.H Graphics, East Sussex (01273) 515527

CONTENTS

FOREWORD

The action which makes a man or woman a hero is as varied as the heroes themselves. It might be an act of gallantry in wartime, perhaps single-handedly leading a charge into enemy lines without thought of the risk to life and limb - like some of the VCs described in this book. Or perhaps it's a lifeboat man going out into the teeth of a howling gale, ignoring the likelihood of being crushed alive - like Peter Thomas you'll read about. Or perhaps it might be a whole lifetime totally sacrificing yourself for others like Sue Ryder.

Something in a hero transcends the usual, and makes an ordinary man or woman extraordinary. Such are the Kent men, women (and animals) that you find in this book. Their courage enriches us and makes us proud.

ILLUSTRATIONS

ACKNOWLEDGMENTS

I am indebted to so many Kent librarians that it would perhaps be invidious to name any one person. Kent librarians have suggested names of heroes, given ideas and winkled out any number of books, cuttings, pictures and other information that have contributed hugely to the interest of this book.

My thanks goes to my wife and Chris McCooey for reading the manuscript and offering many useful suggestions.

Rita Mayer, archivist at the RSPCA was able to discover a number of animals that in one way or another deserved to be called heroes and had been awarded medals for gallantry. On another animal story, Barbara Hunt gave me details and a photograph - relating to the remarkable act of bravery carried out by the very small dog called Mouse.

Wilfred Duncombe of the Farningham and Eynssford Local History Society was able to supply some little known connections of William Bligh to the area.

OMF archivist Margaret Dainton, Julia Cameron and Mark Ellis let me have a number of cuttings and a selection of photographs of two of their missionaries, Alfred Bosshardt and Henry Guinness, who spent their last years here - both of whom had led heroic and extraordinary lives on the other side of the world.

Cliff Housley, Regimental Historian of the Sherwood Foresters supplied both information and photographs of one of their soldiers, Captain Henry Brunt VC.

Policemen Kevin Corby and Julian Pegler were frank and moving in their account of an act of daring that had won them both awards for gallantry. Peter Farrell was able to cite other acts of police bravery, which deserved a place in this book.

Peter Elliot, Senior Keeper of Research and Information Services at the RAF Museum at Hendon was able to fill in some vital missing gaps in the story of the test pilot, Neville Duke.

Robin Brooks was almost solely responsible for the information of pictures of two brave - and medal winning - local ladies in the Second World War. These were Josie Fairclough and Daphne Pearson.

In the accounts of bravery by Kent firemen, Roy Humphries was able to supply a copy of a rare wartime photograph taken by Cyril Brown.

Secret agent and Kent-born Colonel Duane Tyrrel Hudson retired to, and died, in South Africa and several of his friends there contributed to the knowledge of his life. These included Genny Coll from Durban, who referred me to Valerie Flessatti, Hudson's daughter, who was helpful in giving information and a photograph. Phyllis Connerty, from the Durban Municipal Library, referred me to a number of contacts, both in Britain and South Africa. My thanks to them all.

Some of the greatest of Kent's unsung heroes are the lifeboat men and Georgette Purches, deputy head of public relations of the Royal National Lifeboat Institute, arranged for me to use the RNLI library and archive in Poole, Dorset. From there I was referred to medal winner and hero, Peter Thomas, from Dungeness in Kent.

The steep rocks near Tunbridge Wells have been the training ground for many famous mountaineers and photographs of Nea Morin here were supplied by her daughter, Lady Evans. Information on three of the climbers featured in this book - Nea Morin, Albert Mummery and John Noel - was supplied by Margaret Ecclestone, librarian at the Alpine Club.

From 1918 until the end of the Second World War, John Lankester Parker was one of the dare-devil test pilots who at the time earned the adulation now paid to pop stars. His daughter, Sally Beckett, has kept his archives and generously supplied me with a photograph and information on her father.

Sharon McLennon, secretary to John Surtees, gave me a number of items on her boss that greatly helped the Surtees chapter.

Jane Anderson from Sue Ryder Care gave helpful information on their founder, Lady Ryder. Judith Hayter Johnson from Kent's Benenden School kindly lent the school's photograph of Sue Ryder receiving an award from the Princess Royal, at Benenden school.

Many things have been written about the 1747 battle between 'General' Sturt and his Goudhurst militia against the notorious Hawkhurst Gang. Some of these accounts may have used more imagination than fact. In his search for the truth, Tom Browning has unearthed a considerable amount of data that puts the record straight. Mr Browning was kind enough to let me use the results of his research for the chapter on Sturt.

I am sure there were others who in some way or another helped the completion of Kent Heroes. If I have forgotten anyone, my sincere apologies...

Bowen Pearse, Cranbrook, October 2002

The Blue-Eyed Samurai

WILLIAM ADAMS (1564-1620)

Seldom has there been a hero more suited to rip-roaring fiction than William Adams, the first Englishman in Japan. He was born in Kent, captain of a supply ship during Drake's defeat of the Spanish Armada, a traveller through half the world's seas and almost the sole survivor on a voyage to reach the unknown 'Japons'. Upon arriving in Japan, he was imprisoned with a daily expectation of crucifixion, but instead of death rose to be the Shogun's right-hand man and a samurai with power of life and death over some 100 villages.

William Adams

No wonder Adams has been the subject of countless articles, stories, biographies, novels, and films and - in the adaptation of James Clavel's best-selling blockbuster, Shogun - the most successful television mini-series ever made.

The flesh and blood William Adams was born in Gillingham in 1564, the same year as his namesake, Shakespeare. It is not known where precisely he was born in Gillingham but recent research suggests that Adams' family may have been living on a hulk, moored in the Medway (as also apparently was Francis Drake's family).

William Adams was baptised in Gillingham Parish Church on September 24th 1564. At the age of 12, he began a 12-year apprenticeship to Master Nicholas Diggines, a shipbuilder at Limehouse. He was taught shipbuilding, astronomy, mathematics and navigation. Historians have been divided about whether Adam's family were rich or poor. Some point out that a lack of knowledge about his origins suggests a family of low status. Others say that the completeness of his education indicates that he had a fairly comfortable family background. We shall probably never know precisely.

On August 20th 1589 Adams married Mary Hyn in the parish church of St Dunstan's, Stepney, and subsequently had a child by her. Mary must have seen little enough of Will, as he joined the navy, acting as master and pilot. At the time of the Spanish Armada, he captained a supply ship in Drake's navy, responsible for provisioning the fleet. For about a dozen or so years, he worked for a company of Barbary merchants until the opening of the Dutch trade with India tempted him: 'To make a little experience of the small knowledge which God had given me in that Indish traffick'.

Since about 1450, European nations had been exploring the world's oceans, in an attempt to reach the riches of the East. Britain had played its part, as did Holland. One of the aims of the European explorers was to find the fabled north-west passage to China.

On June 27th 1598, five ships set sail from Rotterdam with a number of Britons including William Adams, the expedition's pilot, his brother Thomas, Timothy Shotten and a Scot. Like the French Foreign Legion in modern times, the nationality of seafarers mattered little.

They ran into trouble off the coast of Chile where they were involved in skirmishes with both the Spanish and the natives. Two of the ships decided to sail across the Pacific for Japan where they hoped to sell their cargo of cloth. (Another ship made it to Timor, but the Portuguese seized the crew). During their rough passage to Japan, one of the ships was lost and the sole remaining ship, the *de Liefde* (Charity), with Adams on board, reached the coast of Japan in Bungo Province, near present day Oita City, on April 19th 1600. Only 24 members of the crew had survived.

Japan already had a number of Spanish and Portuguese priests who had converted many to Catholicism; Spain and Portugal also enjoyed exclusive trading rights to Japan. These Catholics had little love for Protestant Holland and England, and did their best to have the newcomers put to death as dangerous intruders. Adams and his crew were treated well at first then imprisoned until the shogun, supreme military dictator, Tokugawa Ieyasu, decided what to do with them. Adams was incarcerated for six weeks, where he was treated well but lived in constant dread of the popular form of execution: crucifixion (another foreign import they had learned from the teachings of the missionaries).

But Ieyasu refused to punish somebody who had done him no wrong and would have nothing to do with European quarrels. He restored Adams to his companions and ordered that the foreigners were to have a daily ration of rice and a small pension.

Ieyasu realised Adams had practical skills and knew that the English pilot had much useful information to tell him. In fact, he found it most interesting that Europe was not the peaceful unified whole he had previously learned from the Catholics.

Within a remarkably short time, Adams was at first released and later became close adviser to the shogun. From this position of trust, Adams taught the Japanese much about shipbuilding and mathematics.

Adams set down how he came to build a small ship of 80 tons for the shogun: 'By which means I came in more favour with him, so that I came often into his presence, who from time to time give me presents and at length a yearly stipend to live upon, much about 70 ducats by the year with two pounds of rice a day, daily. Now being in such grace and favour, by reason I learned him some points of geometry and understanding of the art of mathematics with other things, I pleased him so that what I said he would not contrary'.

Adams built a second ship of 110 tons, which was sea-worthy enough to carry home the Spanish governor of the Philippine Islands, who was wrecked on the coast of Japan.

Eventually, Adams was made a samurai, the highest social rank in Japan, and given a small estate at Hemimura near Yokosuka consisting of about 100 farms over which he exercised dominion like a daimyo (a feudal lord). 'Like a lordship in England', Adams later wrote.

In 1605, Adams and some of his Dutch shipmates became involved in a religious argument with Rodrigues, a Jesuit who acted as court interpreter a post he had also held under the previous shogun, Hideyoshi. The argument was inconclusive and Adams was called an: 'Obstinate heretic who was a man of fine spirit and without having been a student tried to prove his errors by the authority of the same Scripture wrongly interpreted'. Adams would have taken that as a compliment. Certainly, he was a heretic in Spanish eyes but a man of natural talent. When Rodrigues was expelled from Japan in 1610, Adams took over his job of interpreter.

Adams neither liked nor respected the Catholic priests in Japan. He would not easily forget that it was the Jesuits who had first attempted to have him and his crew executed on his arrival. In 1606, there were about 120 Jesuits and some 30 Franciscans in Japan. They had made a number of converts, including some highly placed nobility but the total number of Christians in the country constituted a very low percentage.

Adams told Ieyasu that in Protestant Europe, Catholics were seen as spies and executed. At that stage of the Reformation, Protestantism was not a proselytizing religion. Adams was thus able to tell Ieyasu with perfect honesty that establishing trading links with Holland and England would not be an open door for Protestant missionaries. (That would come several centuries later in the late 19th century).

It took about a year for word of the *Liefde's* fate to reach Holland and England. The news was brought by two of Adams' shipmates who, at Adams' intercession, were permitted to leave Japan. They carried with them letters from the shogun, inviting the Dutch to set up a trading factory in Japan. Holland responded by sending two ships to Hirado in 1609. The Dutch factory was set up there in 1611. Adams was responsible for helping to arrange very favourable terms for the Dutch.

Coincidentally, before Adams' letters reached his home country, England was thinking about setting up trade links with Japan. It was thought to be rich in silver; and would also provide excellent access to the rich pickings to be had from China. Japan was also thought of as a good setting-off-point for the search for the ever-elusive North-West Passage. In 1611, the English East India Company finally decided to send an expedition to Japan to establish an English trading factory there. On April 19th 1611, the *Clove* sailed for Japan, under the command of Captain John Saris.

Adams wrote to Saris at Bantan but Saris had left before the letter arrived. In the letter, Adams advised Saris to set up the factory at Urago, near Edo (modern day Tokyo) and not in Hirado (now in Nagasaki prefecture) where the Dutch were already established. As it turned out, Saris chose Hirado and historians have since criticised the decision: if the company had followed Adams' advice, the factory may not have been the failure it turned out to be. This is in fact unfair. The British East India Company saw Japan as a staging post for the trade with China. The Urago site would have meant much longer sailing times from South-East Asia.

The *Clove* arrived in the harbour of Hirado on June 12th, 1613. Adams was summoned but didn't reach his fellow-countrymen until July 29th. The meeting was somewhat strained. Adams annoyed the English by refusing to stay in their house rather than his own. On August 6th, Saris and Adams together with nine other Englishmen, set out for Ieyasu's court. The meeting went very well. Adams transcribed the letter from King James into Japanese and managed to obtain very good terms for the

East India Company.

Saris, acting on instructions from his employers, offered Adams a passage home. Adams declined - although Ieyasu had at last given his permission - and it's easy to speculate on a number of reasons why. Adams had a wife and two children in Japan. He never really got on with Saris and resented the way he had been treated. He had made very little money and at the age of 49 would not have found it easy to get a job in England. He was also very pleased with his life in Japan - he would hardly have been a lord back home. He still hoped to find the legendary north-west passage to England. And lastly, he had a genuine desire to be useful to the East India Company.

There was prolonged, acrimonious argument between Adams and Saris about many things but particularly as to what part Adams was to play in his employment with the company. After a lot of haggling, a sum of £100 a year was fixed for Adams' salary.

Saris spoke disparagingly about Adams to the head of the English factory, Richard Cocks. Adams was not to be trusted with money; he was only fit to be 'master of a junk' (i.e. for short voyages to Siam) and to be used as an interpreter at court when there was nothing for him to do at sea. This of course contrasted markedly with the opinion Ieyasu had of Adams. Saris simply never got on with Adams and jealousy may also have played a part.

In 1616, Ieyasu died and he was succeeded by his son, Hidetada, who was not impressed by Adams in particular or by foreigners in general. The persecution of Christians, which had almost died out, was now renewed with increased violence. The English factory, having gone through many vicissitudes, was now dissolved. To make matters worse, the Dutch declared war, took English shipping and attacked the factory. Peace was hardly restored when, on May 16th 1620, Adams died.

Adams left an estate of about £500, which was to be divided equally between his families in Japan and England. He was buried on his estate, overlooking the harbour of Yokosuka.

Adams' memory has lived on in Japan and in his birthplace in Kent. Gillingham has an impressive William Adams Memorial and Clock, unveiled by Ambassador Tsuneo Matsudaira in May 1934, located in Watling Street, now part of the main A2. Since April 1982, there has been a twinning arrangement between Adams' 'home town' in Japan, Yokusuka and Gillingham. And in the previous month, the Japanese company, Mitsui, gave the town 38 Japanese painted maples, horse chestnuts and nettle trees.

In 1872, a James Walter discovered Adams' Japanese tomb, which he shared with his Japanese wife. There is a street in Tokyo, Anjin Cho (Pilot Street). And an annual celebration is still held in memory of the Englishman who, in Richard Cocks' words was: 'In such favour with two emperors [shoguns] of Japan as never was any Christian in these parts of the world'.

✳ ✳ ✳

Animal Rescue Heroes

THE RSPCA FILES ARE CRAMMED WITH HEROES - SOME HUMAN,
SOME ANIMAL. HERE A FEW EXCEPTIONAL STORIES FROM KENT.

SAVED FROM DEATH OR CAPTURE

The first incident concerns a Labrador cross collie called Bob, during
the Second World War in North Africa. The dog joined C Company, 6th
Royal West Kent's as a Patrol Dog, after leaving the Army Dogs' Training
School. Bob sailed with the regiment to North Africa and did excellent
work guarding stores and accompanying patrols. He won his Dicken
Medal - the animal's so-called VC - at Green Hill, North Africa, when a
patrol was sent into enemy lines.

Accompanying the men on patrol, Bob stopped in his tracks, giving
warning that enemy troops were near. The patrol leader waited, then
decided to continue but the dog wouldn't budge. A few moments later,
something or someone moved a few yards in front. Bob's timely warning
had saved the patrol from possible death or capture.

Bob continued right through the Sicilian and Italian campaigns. In
cold weather, he wore a warm coat bearing the regimental crest and his
owner's rank. While being returned to England where his owner, R
Cleggett, had been demobbed, Bob slipped his collar in Milan. Every
effort was made to find him but sadly, without success.

OVER THE CLIFF AT DOVER

An 18-year-old soldier, Gunner R Waite, risked serious injury when he
was lowered by rope down the cliff face at East Cliff, Dover. A dog had
fallen and landed on a ledge 10 feet down. While carrying out the rescue,
he was showered with loose chalk. Waite was awarded the RSPCA Bronze
Medal, reported in the *Animal World* of August 1951.

THROUGH SMOKE AND FLAMES

Robert Hacking was gardener and handyman at Smeeth Hill House,
Smeeth, Ashford, Kent, and in charge of three dogs. Two were black
Labradors (one totally blind) and one an Australian Terrier. In the early
evening in February 1963, he opened the back doors of the main house to
give the dogs their dinner. A cloud of thick, dense smoke billowed out.

Disregarding his own safety and thinking only of the welfare of the
dogs, he faced the stifling cloud and went into the house. He switched on
the electric light but little illumination penetrated the smokey gloom.

The sitting room was ablaze. Hacking tried to limit the spread of the fire by closing doors. He ran to where the dogs usually slept but they were not there. Fear had driven them up the stairs away from the fire. At first he was unable to locate them until he heard whining coming from the upper landing.

He called the fire brigade, then dashed upstairs to find the three dogs cowering at the bathroom door. Carefully, he took the blind dog into his arms, as heavy as it was. Then, doing his best with feet and legs, he herded the other two dogs down the stairs and towards the front door. He was unfamiliar with the lock and it took some time to get it open. All the time, he kept trying to calm the dogs.

The strain proved all too much and upon at last opening the door and moving into the fresh air, he collapsed.

Because of the fumes and smoke he had inhaled, he was in a delirium all night and didn't properly recover for several days.

When news of this remarkable story of personal sacrifice reached the awards committee of the RSPCA, an emergency meeting was called. To acknowledge the debt of gratitude owed to this courageous man by all animal lovers, it was decided to award him the coveted RSPCA Silver Medal.

Animal Hero Mighty Mouse

A MIGHTY MIDGET

This story concerns the smallest heroine in the book, a Chihuahuah puppy which went by the grand name of Lady de Mouse of Pembury. Mouse had recently been acquired by a Mr. Schooling who lived in a downstairs flat in Molyneux Park Road, Tunbridge Wells. The upstairs was occupied by the Farrels, who were the owners of the whole house

On a fateful night in 1970, Mr. Farrel half woke to find that Mouse had climbed the stairs and was on his bed, trying to wake him. Still half asleep, Farrel told Mouse to 'shut up' and 'go away'. But still Mouse persevered. At last the tiny puppy managed to fully rouse Farrel. It was as well she did so for the sound sleepers now found that the house was on fire!

Within minutes, everyone was got out of both flats, just in the nick of time. Had the Farrels gone on sleeping another five minutes, it would probably have been too late to escape.

Some time later, at a special animal service on Rusthall Common (where owners brought their pets to be blessed) Mouse was presented with what is referred to as the RSPCA VC. The RSPCA man holding the service said admiringly: 'She's mighty small even for a mighty small breed. And mighty brave too'. The full story was carried by the *Daily Express*.

Mouse, who grew to weigh 5 lbs as a small creamy white adult bitch, lived on with the Farrels to the grand old age of 16. She died in 1986.

THE FIREMAN WHO GAVE HIS LIFE FOR A CAT

The RSPCA's highest award - The Margaret Wheatley Cross - was awarded posthumously to Leading Fireman Roy Chapman for a rescue in July 1980. The award is given in recognition of outstanding bravery in the rescue or attempted rescue of an animal.

In this case, a Tonbridge cat had been marooned for three days in a tree, 35 ft up and had defied all attempts at rescue. Mr. Chapman, a fireman for eight years, volunteered to go up the tree after it. He managed to get on the same branch and to coax the cat into a bag. But the branch was not strong enough for the fireman's weight. There was a sickening crash and both plunged to the tarmac roadway below.

Chapman died of his injuries a week later. The cat survived.

Not The Man You Thought Him To Be.

WILIAM BLIGH (1753-1817)

Captain William Bligh

History and Hollywood have given William Bligh - who retired to the Manor House in Farningham in Kent - a very bad press. Seen through the brilliant acting of Charles Laughton or Trevor Howard, he was a cruel, sadistic tyrant. But in real life, Bligh was humane and just - certainly, as judged by 18th century standards.

In a long and distinguished naval career, in which the *Bounty* experience was but a short interlude, his log shows great concern for his men. Conditions on sailing ships were appalling and Bligh always did his utmost to make them better. Bligh's record of punishments was one of the lowest of any ship in the fleet. And this was true of every ship he commanded.

Out of the *Bounty* experience came Bligh's greatest challenge. As most readers and cinemagoers will remember, he was put into a small lifeboat with 18 men, few provisions, and no navigational aids. He was expected to perish. But instead, he made the voyage of 3,618 miles to Timor, in some three months. Such a navigational feat has seldom been equalled in naval history. To achieve this, he showed extraordinary courage and exemplary seamanship.

William Bligh was baptised at St Andrew's Church, Plymouth, on October 4th, 1754. He was the only son of Francis Bligh, of Tynten (or Tinten). It was an old family; one ancestor had been a hatchet man for the suppression of the monasteries under Henry VIII.

'Breadfruit Bligh', as he was nicknamed, having joined the navy, sailed with Captain Cook on his second voyage around the world in 1772-4. His position was sailing-master on the *Resolution* and it was on this trip that breadfruit was discovered in Tahiti. Bligh became a lieutenant and made several important hydrographic surveys. He was involved in the battle off the Doggerbank on August 5th 1781, against the Dutch, in the American Revolutionary War, and served under Lord Howe at Gibraltar in 1782. He had already made a name for himself as a skilful navigator before being appointed to captain the Bounty in December 1787.

The *Bounty* left Portsmouth with a company of 62 men. Among them of course was Fletcher Christian, something of a protégé of Bligh; the two had sailed together previously on the *Britannic*. In the ship's log, it will be seen that the captain did his best to keep the men fit and in good spirits. His experience with Cook had shown him the practical advantage of this.

The *Bounty* reached Tahiti after ten months sailing and it was here that the trouble began. After the rigours of shipboard life, it must have seemed like an island paradise - with little to do but swim, lie in the sun, and be served by compliant, dusky Tahitian women. Each of the crew took several mistresses - Christian had six! After five or six months there, it was time to go and several men deserted. In evidence of his benign nature, Bligh pardoned the deserters only to make trouble for himself later - for these men were among the ringleaders of the mutiny to come.

On board ship, the crew became increasingly difficult to control and - much against his nature - the rulebook dictated that harsh physical punishment was called for. But the floggings only increased the general resentment. On April 28th 1789, under the leadership of Fletcher Christian, the majority of the crew took over the ship, casting Bligh and the crewmembers loyal to him off in a lifeboat.

The mutineers returned to Tahiti, collected their women and provisions and began their search for a suitable island to colonise. This was eventually found on Pitcairn, where their descendants live today, happy and prosperous, still speaking the English dialect of the 18th century.

Bligh on the other hand navigated his frail craft to far away Timor, near Java, arriving on June 14th 1789. They had managed to pick up water and meagre rations from several islands along the way and arrived with provisions for only another 11 days. During all this time, it is reported that Bligh's self-sacrifice and devotion to his men was little short of heroic.

The Dutch settlers in nearby Java were most helpful, dressing their sores and providing food, clothes and accommodation. When he was fit enough, Bligh used his commission to purchase a small schooner and supplies to get them to Batavia, where sea passages were taken back to Europe.

At home, Bligh was completely exonerated from any blame and promoted to the rank of commander, later to post-captain. A number of mutineers were found still living in Tahiti. They were rounded up, returned to England and executed.

In 1791 Bligh was appointed to the *Providence,* on which he had a most successful voyage to the Society Islands. For the work there, he was awarded the Gold Medal of the Society of Arts in 1794.

There followed a number of naval commands. In 1794, he was made captain of the 74-gun ship *Warrior.* In 1797, at Camperdown, he commanded the 64-gun *Director* and helped to settle the complicated machinations of the Nora Mutiny. On May 21st 1801, Bligh commanded the *Glatton* against the Danes, in the Battle of Copenhagen. Admiral Nelson thanked him personally - an honour Bligh always treasured. In the same year, he was elected a Fellow of the Royal Society, for his considerable services in navigation and botany.

Life was seldom calm for long and in 1805, Bligh was appointed captain-general and governor of the newly established penal colony of New South Wales. He soon came into conflict with some of the leaders of the free community, mainly in his opposition to the flourishing rum trade. On January 26th 1808, Governor Bligh was forcibly deposed and imprisoned until March 1810. The man responsible, Major George Johnson, was tried at Chelsea Hospital in 1811 and dismissed from the service with dishonour.

On his return to England in 1811, Bligh was created rear admiral of the blue, rising to vice-admiral of the blue in June 1814 (blue being the most junior rank in comparison with the ranks of the red and the white).

It must have been a great regret to Bligh that his wife, Elizabeth, was unable to share his retirement. She was a highly intelligent woman, whose father was a scholar and friend of such men as Adam Smith, the economist. Elizabeth died on April 15th 1812 and was buried in the family grave at Lambeth Churchyard.

Soon after this, Bligh went to live at the imposing Manor House in Farningham, in Kent, with his unmarried daughters. He must have known the district quite well as he had stayed with distant relatives at Cobham Hall when he was young, between voyages. The country life suited him well for he wrote warmly to his friend and patron, Sir Joseph Banks.

He told Banks he loved both the house and the surrounding Kent countryside. 'It is a good and hospitable mansion where I have felt a hearty welcome and have the benefit of walking about all these grounds without control, in the midst of pleasant fine country, breathing the purest air, improving my daughters very much in health.' He appears to have been no recluse but quite involved in parish affairs; there is a report in the local archives citing Bligh as one of a number of men walking the bounds of Farningham in 1816, a year before he died.

A souvenir of his heroic voyage from the *Bounty* survived with him. It was a pistol ball, with which he had weighed the rations in the little boat in which he had been cast adrift - so as to be fair to all. Visiting children would love it when he produced the ball and begged him once again to tell the story of his epic voyage. And it wasn't just children who listened spellbound.

As business and health permitted, William Bligh travelled up to London and it was on one of these trips that he collapsed and died in Bond Street, on December 7th 1817. He was buried beside his wife. The inscription on his tombstone reads:

Sacred
to the Memory of
William Bligh Esq., F.R.S.
Vice Admiral of the Blue
the celebrated navigator
who first transplanted the Bread fruit tree
from Otaheite [Tahiti] to the West Indies
bravely fought the battles of his country
and died beloved, respected and lamented
on the 7th day of December 1817
aged 64

William Bligh has had much mud slung in his direction but what was the man really like - hero or tyrant? His biographer, Gavin Kennedy, sums him up in this way: '...there were many who would swear he was the best there was when other men (more saintly perhaps) would have been overwhelmed.

'He was a fighter, a survivor, a man of intense personal conviction and also a man of considerable courage. His critics claimed he was a bully, a tyrant, a coward and a thief. I am one observer who firmly believes that they were unjust.'

William Bligh was a hero, in the very best sense of the word.

✳ ✳ ✳

2,500-Miles March to Freedom

ALFRED BOSSHARDT (1897-1993)

On October 1st 1934, Alfred and Rose Bosshardt, a missionary couple in China, were returning home to their village, Zhenyuan, in Guizhou province. They had been working in the country for over ten years and were concerned about bandits and Communists, known to be active in the area. The Red Army had decimated the missionary community, supposing them all to be imperialist spies. Alfred and his wife knew that if they were captured, they would most likely be imprisoned or put to death.

Alfred Bosshardt as a young man

Which route should they take? They decided on the newer, shorter road, which should be better guarded by government troops. They started along it, making for the village in which they planned to stay the night. As they went up the last hill before they reached their destination, armed men sprang from the bushes and took them prisoner. The result was to be separation and - for Alfred - some 18 months of pain and degradation, from which he almost died.

Most people would have said they took the wrong road. But for Alfred and Rose, it was a matter of faith. Despite all that they had had to go through, to the end of their lives they maintained the choice was in God's hands. Looked at in these terms, it was the right decision. Such was their faith.

The Red Army was composed of several fighting groups, which broke out of the Nationalist encirclement in the south. Mao Tse-tung eventually commanded the main First Front Army, which reached its final destination, Shanxi, first. Alfred, along with a New Zealander, Arnolis

Hayman, was captured by the Second Front Army, led by He Long and Xiao Ke.

Alfred Bosshardt - who spent his last years in Pembury - was born in Manchester on January 1st 1897, of Swiss Baptist parents. At the age of ten, he felt the call of the Far East, after hearing a speech by a China missionary, 'who spoke Chinese with the barest trace of a Lancashire accent'.

After completing an apprenticeship in engineering in 1922, he approached the China Inland Mission (now OMF International). He was accepted and sent to Kweichow Province, a mountainous region with no roads, about the size of England. He travelled bare-foot and dressed in Chinese costume, as was the custom of the mission society.

In 1925, there was a severe famine in the area and Bosshardt almost died of typhoid. However, he made a good recovery and met Rose Piaget, a fellow Swiss and daughter of a watchmaker. They were married in 1931.

On that fateful day in October 1934, their Communist captors soon freed Rose and also freed Arnolis Hayman's family. But the two men were held for a ransom of $100,000. Alfred and Arnolis now became amongst the few Europeans - mainly missionary captives - who took part in the famous 6,000 miles trek, which changed China's history. About 100,000 Communists set off from south-east China, across trackless wastes, armed only with rudimentary weapons and no motorised transport. Only about 5,000 eventually reached Shanxi, some 6,000 miles to the north-west.

Conditions were appalling with frequent air and land attacks from Chiang Kai-shek's Nationalist forces. The marchers suffered extreme privations of hunger, cold and exhaustion. They had to trudge non-stop, day and night across rivers, swamps and snow-covered mountains in some of the roughest terrain in East Asia. Temperatures were well below freezing. At night they slept in their clothes, often frozen stiff, in conditions so cramped it was impossible to lie flat.

Yet in a letter smuggled out to his wife, Alfred wrote: 'We have passed through magnificent country ... as our days, so has our strength been, and will be'. It was this undiminished faith that saw him through. He was even able to feel compassion for his captors.

Using a sword, he fashioned a crochet hook from a chopstick and with this made woollen caps and gloves for his guards. He saw all as being common sufferers. He later recalled that: 'In such bleak conditions, captives and captors have much in common. At the frontiers of endurance, men cling together in a common struggle for survival'.

The Chinese maps used in the Long March were those produced for schools and were strategically useless. In Guizhou, they were able to buy

French maps of the area. Alfred proved his worth by translating the French into Chinese.

At the time they set out, they were forced to stand and watch the beheading of two young American missionaries; Chinese landlords and other 'class enemies' were routinely beheaded by teenage Communist peasant boys.

Alfred was arraigned as an 'imperialist spy' before a howling Communist mob in a town square. Time after time, he was sentenced to death, as the demanded ransoms weren't paid. Once he escaped, was recaptured and severely beaten with bamboo sticks.

The two missionaries were threatened with further cruel beatings and a definite date was finally set for their execution if their ransom of $100,000 was not paid. The mission was supposed to provide a variety of things, from guns to medicine. Over the months, one deal after another was proposed. At last, when a number of coolies arrived with sacks of silver, the Communists went back on their word and released only Arnolis Hayman.

Alfred was finally released in Kunming on Easter Sunday 1936, having walked some 2,500 miles. He was suffering from pleurisy, bronchitis, beri-beri and two sub-tropical diseases. Had he not been released when he was, doctors said he would have died within days. Rose flew out to meet him and the couple came to Britain before returning to rural China to settle. While recovering from his ordeal, Alfred wrote an account of his experiences called *The Restraining Hand*; this was followed in the 1970s by a fuller autobiography, *The Guiding Hand*.

In 1989, *The Guiding Hand* was translated into Chinese and published in Beijing. The most celebrated survivor of the Long March, General Xiao Ke, wrote a preface in which he

Alfred Bossenhardt returning from captivity in 1936

admitted that the Red Army had been wrong to treat all foreign missionaries as spies.

The book has subsequently been used for instruction in the Peking National Defence University. A recent film has been made of the book, in Mandarin, produced by the Sian Film Studio with a screenplay by the Chinese dramatist, Zheng Zhong.

When the Bosshardts returned to China, it was to Panhsien. They received permission to visit the men and women's prisons. Conditions were extremely harsh and those without relatives to bring them food were left to starve. Alfred begged the chief magistrate to allow them to bring the rice water that was thrown away. This was granted and after that the Bosshardts brought two pails to the prison every day.

Under the Communists, beggars were recruited as spies. Accusations by one person against another undermined all trust and suicides were a frequent occurrence. The Bosshardt's church was not closed but great pressure was brought on Christians to renounce their faith. Only one of Bosshardt's congregation did this - a mother who had been brain washed by her Red Army son.

By 1951, all missionaries were expelled from China. Rather than return to England, Alfred and Rose moved to Pakse in Laos, where they ministered to Mandarin speaking Chinese. Here too they were seen as spies and much patient work was needed to win the people over. Alfred began with the children who were naturally drawn to him. He could make a mouse out of a handkerchief and make it jump. Youths came to Alfred to learn English and he used the Bible as the main text. Gradually, one by one, the people came to trust the two missionaries.

Rose suffered from declining health and they planned a return to England. But then in May 1965, Rose died and Alfred buried her amongst the community they had both come to love. Alfred decided to stay on a little longer.

In the following year, he returned to Manchester where he did much fine work in the Chinese Christian church. Eventually he helped it to become the second biggest Chinese Christian community in Britain.

In the 1980s Alfred made contact with General Xiao Ke, the Chinese commander of the section of the army that had taken him prisoner and China's greatest surviving hero of the Long March. The two men exchanged messages, following a chance remark by an American writer to Xiao Ke that his old prisoner was still alive in England. Shortly before he died, Alfred wrote that friendly links with this man had been: 'A source of great pleasure'.

In 1990, after the outbreak of a mysterious paralysis that doctors attributed to his deprivation on the Long March, it was necessary for Alfred to have full-time nursing care. He moved to Cornford House, in Cornford Lane, a nursing home in Pembury, Kent, run by OMF. He died there on November 6th 1993.

Anthony Grey, the former Reuters' correspondent who was held captive by the Red Guards during the Cultural Revolution, called Alfred: 'Perhaps the most saintly individual I've ever met. In the horror of the Long March he put aside all thoughts of hatred and told himself: "God loves these people, so I must love them too". This fundamental essence of Christian teaching clearly informed the whole of his remarkable life'.

Fastest Man on Land and Water

MALCOLM CAMPBELL (1885-1948)

Sometime in 1901, down a busy street in Bickley Hill, Bromley, Kent, a 16-year-old lad rode a bicycle at speed down the steep slope, with his hands nonchalantly stuffed into his pockets. He succeeded in terrifying two old ladies and at the subsequent hearing at the Bromley Police Court, the policemen claimed the speed was 27mph and the rider, Malcolm Campbell, was fined £1.50 - a considerable sum back at the beginning of the last century. But Malcolm Campbell - perhaps the greatest name in early speed-making - was no ordinary teenager. And never has a magistrate's admonition - not to travel so fast in future - been so magnificently disobeyed.

In his autobiographical *Speed on Wheels,* Malcolm attempts to define 'the lure of speed'. He writes that it is 'an urge that most civilised human beings feel...you have this longing, this insatiable urge in your system'. In

Sir Malcolm Campbell in 1935

himself, he sees a 'craving [that] has kept on going, growing and growing and like some diseases, has become stronger and stronger as time passes.'

Malcolm, later Sir Malcolm Campbell, was born in Chislehurst, Kent, on March 11th 1885, the only son and elder child of William Campbell, a wealthy watchmaker and jeweller, of Cheapside. (The family was proud of the fact that they descended from a Campbell who had fought at Culloden.)

The young Malcolm was educated at Uppingham and in Germany and France. He spurned the family business for a life of speed but his father insisted that, at least, he get a profession.

So at the age of 21, Malcolm became an underwriting member of Lloyds. One of his best ideas in this field was to insure newspapers against libel - a very profitable concern until other insurers took up the idea and provided competition. In subsequent years, his passion for racing brought in extra income - as in 1909, for example, he made £750 by underwriting Louis Bleriot against risk when the Frenchman made his first cross-Channel flight. The plane was later on show in an Oxford Street store, where Malcolm made careful notes for creating his own aeroplane.

With the aid of these notes, he designed and built a monoplane in a disused barn and he and a friend rolled it out onto a strawberry field near Orpington in Kent. People gathered round, making disparaging remarks and didn't even bother to get out of the way as the engine spluttered to life and the plane started moving in their direction. All Malcolm could see was a group of frightened faces as he yanked back the joystick. At the first attempt, the plane flew, stalled, nose-dived and crashed. It was repaired and he flew it again for all of 100-yards. Perhaps these experiences should really qualify the pilot as one of Britain's first flyers.

Some years earlier, Malcolm bought his first land vehicle, a second-hand, 1902 3¼hp Rex motor-bike, for £15 from the Vivid Motor Works, in East Street, Bromley. He crashed into his own front fence, landing him on the lawn. His first car came from the same garage, a 20hp Germain. The car stranded him at Westerham with 'engine trouble'. Called to do the repair, the garage found that the petrol tap had been turned off!

He began competition racing with motor bikes, ever bigger and more powerful. In 1906, he achieved his first success with a gold medal in the London to Lands End trials. The next two years brought him two similar gold medals.

Around this time, he switched from racing motor-bikes to racing cars. He participated in his first race at Brooklands, the early racing-car track in Surrey, a year after its opening date of 1907. In 1910, he bought a big Darracq, which had won the Vanderbilt Cup in America the previous year and was capable of 100mph.

He was about to paint it 'Flapper III' (a name he had given his earlier vehicles) when he changed his mind and christened it the 'Bluebird', from Maeterlinck's play, then having a good run in the West End of London. He bought some paint and sat up half the night painting the car blue. It won the race for him the following morning and from that time on he named all his cars (and ultimately his racing boats) 'Bluebird'. Malcolm and his 'Bluebirds' became well known in his home town of Bromley. He would roar out of the Bromley Motor Works, turn right up Masons Hill and put the car through its paces in Oakley Road, Bromley Common.

In 1912, he suffered the first of his near-escapes-from-death in the same 'Bluebird' and the track at Brooklands. Speeding at over a mile-and-a-half a minute, the car lost both its front and rear wheels almost simultaneously. It slewed sideways on its two clattering hubs as Malcolm struggled to wrench the car onto the edge of the track and shot over the finishing line, fourth in the race.

With the outbreak of the First World War in 1914, he enlisted as a dispatch rider and was soon commissioned by the Royal West Kent Regiment and transferred to the Royal Flying Corps. From 1916 to the end of the war, he served first as a ferry pilot and then as a flying instructor. He was demobbed as a captain and an MBE.

Like many people, he dreamed of having a business that was closely connected to his interests and passions. The motoring trade was an obvious choice and he tinkered around with several car-selling ventures, all of which failed disastrously. On the lookout for something else, he hit upon the idea of finding hidden treasure - pirate's gold. He bought all the books he could find on the subject and even led a party to the Cocos Islands in search of the buried treasure reputed to be there - but he was no more successful in this than he had been in selling cars.

In 1920, he married Dorothy Evelyn, daughter of Major William Whittall. Dorothy wrote the autobiographical *Malcolm Campbell, the Man as I Knew Him,* published in 1951. It is a revealing insight. Dorothy described a quite different man from that worshipped by his many fans, a much more difficult man who drove all three of his wives to leave him. Marriages to the first and third wives were dissolved after a short period. Dorothy, number two, also left the marriage but nevertheless remained a friend to the end.

It is not easy to see why Dorothy stuck to him so long. Among many things, she accuses him of infidelity. She writes that he was very attractive to women and felt sure he had had numerous affairs. He could also be extraordinarily selfish and hard hearted. When Dorothy was about to have a baby and in need of both comfort and the midwife fetched quickly, Malcolm went off to build a dog kennel, ignoring his wife's pleas.

As Dorothy describes him, Malcolm was like a small boy constantly discovering new crazes. He would pursue the current craze for a while at the expense of everything else - then drop it and start another. These included an expensive and extensive model train set, a library of specialist books, and various collections of such things as chinaware. As another kind of 'Malcolm craze', he even felt it his patriotic duty to stand as a Conservative candidate for Depford in 1935: he was not successful.

Sir Malcolm Campbell at Daytona, 1935

But no matter how difficult he was, Dorothy always had the excuse: Malcolm was no ordinary man. And almost to the end, she forgave him everything.

Despite numerous hair-breadth escapes from death, he won more than 400 trophies, including the 200-mile race at Brooklands in 1927 and 1928, and the Boulogne grand prix in 1927. He outgrew Brooklands and looked all over the world for long flat areas on which he could reach very high speeds. There were many discoveries but just as many disappointments. One perfect location was suggested in Africa - until it was found that it would have been almost impossible to transport the car to the site; it was near neither road nor train line.

Between 1924 and 1935, he raised the speed record nine times. He reached 246.09mph at Daytona Beach, Florida, in 1931, a feat for which he was given a triumphal progress through London to Westminster Hall and the honour of a knighthood. In 1932, he raised the record again to over 250mph. Finally in 1935, in a Rolls-Royce-Campbell, he reached 301.13mph on the Bonneville salt-flats in Utah, in America. Having achieved so much, he seemed at last content to leave the land record where he had put it - unless it was beaten by a foreigner.

However, he now found a new outlet for his passion for speed. He would build a motor-boat that would make him the fastest man on water as well as the land. In 1937, he had his first Bluebird boat built with a Rolls-Royce aero-engine and had it shipped to Lake Maggiore in Italy. A few days after this, Malcolm beat the existing world record of 124.86mph with a speed of 129.5mph. In the following year, he improved on his own record with 130.86mph on Lake Hallwill, in Switzerland. Determined to improve on this again, he had yet another Bluebird built, also with a Rolls-Royce engine. Just before the outbreak of war in 1939, he took the new craft to Coniston Water, where he reached a speed of 141.7mph. For this achievement, in the following year, he was awarded the trophy founded in the memory of his close rival, Sir Henry Segrave.

In a small way, Malcolm also made his name as a writer. He contributed various articles to *The Field* and to the *Daily Mail*. He also authored a number of books on motoring and his joy of speed.

After the Second World War, he made another attempt on the world speed record on water but was unsuccessful. By this time, he was a sick man. His eyesight was failing and he had had a slight stroke. However he kept up a punishing pace of work, despite doctor's orders to slow down. Had he heeded this advice, Dorothy believed, he would not have died at the young age of 63.

But there have been other speed kings pushing up the records since Malcolm's death. The land record now stands at an astonishing 763mph, achieved by Andy Green, in his car, Thrust, on the Black Rock Desert, Nevada, in the U.S, on October 15th 1997. The water record was made in October 1978, by Ken Warby, in his hydroplane, The Spirit of Australia. He reached 317.55mph, on Blowering Dam Lake, New South Wales.

Wouldn't Malcolm have been envious!

✳ ✳ ✳

First of the Few

HUGH CASSWALL TREMENHEERE 1ST BARON DOWDING (1882-1970)

'As England, despite her hopeless military situation, still shows no sign of willingness to come to terms, I have decided to prepare, and if necessary to carry out, a landing operation against her...

'The aim of this operation is to eliminate the English motherland as a base from which war against Germany can be continued and if necessary to occupy the country completely.'

Adolf Hitler, Directive No 16, 16 July 1940

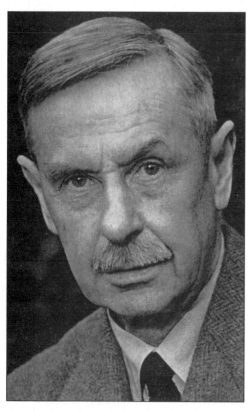

Air Chief Marshall Lord Dowding

In the summer of 1940, in the skies above Kent and Sussex, a battle took place that was to change the course of history. For a few agonising weeks, the fate of the free world hung in the balance. The victory in the Battle of Britain was achieved in no small part, by the genius and stubbornness of one man - Sir Hugh Dowding, Commander in Chief, Fighter Command (later to become Air Chief Marshal the Lord Dowding) - and the skill, dedication, and courage of the pilots he called his 'chickens'.

These very young pilots have been described as the happiest, brightest company who ever fired their guns in anger. But young as they were, there have seldom been men so highly skilled in the art of killing. And this was what they proved that summer.

Their leader, the excessively reticent Dowding, was a thorough-going, highly professional military airman. For some fourteen months, since the outbreak of war, he had almost single-handedly held the defence of the United Kingdom in his hands. In the end, the Luftwaffe stopped coming in daylight and Hitler abandoned his plans to invade Britain. Then, in the Dowding's hour of triumph, when the cheers of a grateful nation should have rung out loudest, he was sacked from his post.

For years after this, Dowding remained in the shadows. From time to time, lip-service was paid to his achievements but no genuine recognition. In some respects, he brought this upon himself for, in his own words, he had always been 'extremely anxious to avoid any statements on contentious matters.' The subject was so bruising that for a long time he wouldn't discuss the Battle of Britain even with close friends.

The devastating strain suffered by Dowding, defending Britain from air attack, has seldom been aired publicly. But some time before the publication of Robert Wright's 1969 biography, *Dowding and the Battle of Britain,* Dowding wrote to the author of his experiences: 'I was fighting the Germans' he wrote, 'and the French and the Cabinet and the Air Ministry and now and again the Navy for good measure...' The plain evidence that he won these fights is his victory over Hitler. That he subsequently lost his job was his defeat.

Hugh Dowding was born at Moffat, Dumfriesshire, on April 24 1882, the eldest in a family of three boys and one girl, of Arthur John Caswell Dowding, schoolmaster, and his wife, Maud Caroline. He began his education at the successful preparatory school run by his parents, and afterwards, followed his father to Winchester. Unable to get on with Greek verbs, he chose the Army class and later the Royal Military Academy at Greenwich. He was gazetted to the Royal Garrison Artillery and served the empire in Gibralter, Colombo and Hongkong, before transferring to the Mountain Artillery in India, where he spent six happy years. For some time, he had sought to be allowed to sit the staff college entrance exam and was finally able to take a year's furlough to study for it.

He went to the Camberly Staff College during 1912 and 1913, where he acquired (and retained during his career) the nickname of 'Stuffy' - though nobody seemed to know why. It completely belied his gift of charm and accessibility.

Dowding developed a keen interest in flying and - in his own time - learned to fly at Brooklands, the flying school run by the firm of Vickers. His pilot's certificate was obtained on the day of his passing out of college, December 20, 1913. At the conclusion of a three-month course at the Central Flying School at Upavon in Wiltshire, permission was given to transfer to the Royal Flying Corps.

At the outbreak of the First World War, the young officer was given command of the camp from which the first squadrons of the Royal Flying

Corps (RFC) left for France. He served in Belgium and was briefly at the RFC Headquarters in France.

In 1915 Dowding returned home to form the Wireless Experimental Establishment at Brooklands. But after a few months he was back in France. During the Battle of the Somme he was in command of the Ninth (Headquarters) Wing. He was responsible for carrying out the final training of the first squadron of Sopwith aircraft with guns firing through the airscrew.

A misunderstanding arose between Dowding and Trenchard, his commanding officer, who insisted on frequent patrols over enemy territory. Dowding believed this was wrong because of the high casualties and characteristically, was not backward in making his views known. His request that one of his squadrons should be relieved was granted. But he was dismissed from his command and received no further appointment in France. He was sent to Salisbury to run the Southern Training Brigade, where he stayed for the rest of the war. He was, however, promoted to Brigadier-General and was awarded the CMG for his war services.

In 1918, he married Clarice Maud, daughter of Captain John Williams but the marriage was cruelly ended by her death following an operation for appendicitis in 1920. He was left with their baby son, Derek, who, 20 years later, became a Wing Commander in the RAF.

Despite his wartime experience and elevation to Brigadier-General, when the Royal Air Force was first formed, Dowding was not immediately picked for a commission. The reason for this was probably his old quarrel with Trenchard, who was still in a position of power. However, at the intercession of other officers, Dowding was at last granted the opportunity to join the select band who would lay the foundations of the new service. He organised some of the early Hendon air pageants and served as Chief Staff Officer, first at Uxbridge and then at HQ Iraq - all of which gave him increased opportunities for flying. In 1926, he became director of training at the Air Ministry and at last gained the favourable notice of Trenchard, then chief of air staff. In 1929, he was appointed AOC Transjordan and Palestine - at a time of growing hostility between the Arabs and the Jews. At the end of 1930, he was appointed to the Air Council as Air Member for Supply and Research.

In the building up of the air force, technology became increasingly complex and although Dowding had had no scientific training, he seemed to show a remarkable capacity for understanding what was required. He sought to encourage the development of fighter aircraft and it was largely on his initiative that the Hurricane and Spitfire were ordered in 1934. He also saw the possibilities of radar and did everything to encourage its development.

Dowding had always been forthright and independent and many years after the war, he set down some of his views on paper. He wrote: 'Since I was a child I have never accepted ideas purely because they were orthodox, and consequently I have frequently found myself in opposition to generally accepted views. Perhaps in retrospect, this has not been altogether a bad thing.'

His main concern, however, was the defence of his country against daylight aerial bombardment. And even if he had not lived to direct the Battle of Britain, his service to the air force at this stage would have placed him amongst his country's greatest saviours. When Fighter Command was set up in July 1936, Dowding was the natural choice to become its Commander-in-Chief.

In May 1940, Dowding made one of the most important decisions in his life - and one that probably contributed most to the victory in the Battle of Britain. The government contemplated sending a substantial part of the Royal Air Force to France as a gesture of encouragement to the French. Dowding argued - with an authority no other official could match - that to send his planes into France would not have saved that country but would put at grave risk the defence of his own.

His letter setting out his objections is an important historical document. It concludes: 'If the Home Defence Force is drained away in desperate attempts to remedy the situation in France, defeat in France will involve the final, complete and irremediable defeat of this country.' He reinforced his message with a talk to Churchill's War Cabinet.

Yet it was another month before the matter was resolved - a month during which Dowding saw his resources 'slipping away like sand in an hour-glass' not least during the evacuation of Dunkirk. The RAF's participation here was crucial and Churchill saw it as Dowding's first victory over the Luffwaffe. The losses were great but not mortal. He had retained enough resources to fight the next chapter of the war.

Dowding's use of the RAF was masterly. The deployment of his forces, his rotation of squadrons, which had been heavily engaged, his constant regard for reserves of aircraft and personnel, indicated skill of a high order. The organisation of the enemy was at the other extreme: the Luftwaffe lost the battle through bad senior leadership, faulty tactics and mistaken target selection.

Dowding saw quite clearly that victory at this time would prevent a German invasion by denying the enemy control of the air. But he also saw the war as a fight between good and evil. In his *Twelve Legions of Angels,* a book he wrote during the war setting out his personal philosophy, this is his description of the enemy. 'The Germans', he wrote, 'are not a very decent people. The willing docility of the German people to the aggressive spirit of Prussia has been the standing menace to European peace for the last eighty years. It is immaterial what leader or clique is at the head of the State. If one is destroyed, another will arise. The German nation must be decisively beaten, and made to realise the fact....' The book, however, was suppressed under wartime regulations and not released until 1946.

But while the Battle of Britain was raging by day and eventually won, night bombing of Britain's cities continued unabated. Dowding spent most nights monitoring the development of airborne radar and other techniques. Perhaps because he was so constantly engrossed in tactics of the war, he failed to notice the discontent around him.

Now aged 58 and embarrassingly older than the rest of the High Command, he was being widely criticised. He was seen as somebody who refused to co-operate, and with whom it was difficult to get on. In contrast to Fighter Command's daytime success, at night the Luftwaffe seemed to be having its own way. Of course it was unfair to blame Dowding for this, but there were many who believed it was time for a change. Even Churchill, who believed Dowding was one of his best men, was persuaded to dismiss him - though he admitted 'it broke my heart.' On November 13th 1940, Dowding was relieved of his post

This was a humiliating slap in the face for Dowding. Since July 1938, when he had been told that he would be retired in June 1939, he had been repeatedly invited to extend his service by short periods and on August 12th, 1940, he was asked to remain without time limit.

After leaving Fighter Command, Dowding was given several jobs to do - including a request from Churchill to procure aircraft from the United States. But these were entirely unsuitable for his talents and he retired from the service in 1942. In 1943, he received a barony - and there were many who said that even this honour had been delayed too long.

There had been much controversy at the time of Dowding's dismissal and this was revived in 1957 by the publication of Dowding's authorised biography, *Leader of the Few,* by Basil Collier, with whom Dowding had co-operated fully.

'To many', Collier wrote, 'Dowding's removal from his post immediately after he had won brilliantly, a hard-fought battle, seemed an act of almost monstrous folly and ingratitude.' There were others who felt he should have been promoted to the most senior rank of Marshal of the Royal Air Force, which would have almost doubled his salary.

In 1951, aged nearly 70, he married for a second time to Muriel, widow of Pilot Officer Maxwell Whiting, and moved into her house in Southborough, Kent. She shared his interests and brought him great happiness. Dowding was passionately interested in the welfare of animals and it seems that here too Muriel was of like mind. The story is told that shortly after their wedding, the new husband said to his bride: 'Darling, it can't be true - but I've just counted 13 animals in the house.'

Dowding became a champion of animal welfare on many occasions. On one of his numerous speeches to the House of Lords, he said: 'All life is one, and all its manifestations with which we have contact are climbing the ladder of evolution. The animals are our younger brothers and sisters, also on the ladder, but a few rungs lower down than we are. It is an important part of our responsibilities to help them in their ascent and not to retard their development by cruel exploitation of their helplessness.'

Because of his small appetite and dislike of vegetables, Muriel was reluctant to persuade Dowding to join her in her vegetarianism. But in the end, she didn't need to. In preparation for his speech in the Lords on the Humane Slaughter bill, he made a tour of slaughterhouses in different parts of the country. This so disgusted him that on his return, he said to Muriel: 'Please do not ever give me meat to eat again.'

His speeches in the Lords in the Humane Slaughter bill resulted in legislation which made the stunning of sheep and lambs before killing compulsory throughout the country.

In 1957, he requested an inquiry into the Cruelty to Animals Act and supported many other humane Bills. One was The Protection of Animals (Anaesthetics) Act 1964. Among other things, it prohibited the castration or other operations on farm animals without the use of anaesthetic. Castration was made illegal below the age of six years for horses and under six months for other farm animals.

In September 1969, confined to a wheelchair because of arthritis, the great man arrived at the premiere of the film, *Battle of Britain,* to see Laurence Olivier playing his role. When Dowding entered the cinema, some 1,500 people rose to their feet to give him a tremendous ovation. This was repeated when he left. Among the audience were some 350 of his one-time 'chickens.'

Dowding was a confident speaker and a lucid writer. His nature had always been contemplative and philosophical and his books reflected this. *Many Mansions* was published in 1943, followed by *Lynchgate* (1945),

God's Magic (1946), and *The Dark Star* (1951). He wrote numerous articles for newspapers and gave lectures on the occult. Along with animal welfare, spiritualism became one of the great passions of his last years.

He had long been a spiritualist and became a member of the Theosophical Society. He found in the study of theosophy, a wonderful enlargement of the mind and spirit and devoted some pages of his book, *Lynchgate* to it. However, he disdained the name of theosophist. All his life he had had a mind of his own and protested that if he was any kind of '-ist', he was a Dowdingist. And that about sums him up.

Air Chief Marshall Lord Dowding

A memorial was unveiled to him in Calverley Park, Tunbridge Wells, in 1987 and a street, Dowding Way, also in Tunbridge Wells, was named after the great man in 1989.

On February 15, 1970, Lord Dowding died quietly at his home in Calverley Park, Tunbridge Wells. A distinguished local resident wrote sadly: 'Poor Tunbridge Wells, it has lost the only claim to greatness in this age'. At the Memorial Service in Westminster Abbey, where his ashes are laid, Denis Healey, then Secretary of State for Defence, said: 'Lord Dowding was one of those great men whom this country miraculously produces in times of peril. He occupies a very special place in the hearts of the British people - and rightly so...'

✳ ✳ ✳

No Fear - 'Just An Excited Urge with a Queer Feeling Inside'.

NEVILLE FREDERICK DUKE (1922-)

On the afternoon of September 6th 1952, all eyes at the Farnborough air show were looking expectantly into a clear blue sky. Nobody was prepared for the catastrophe that was about to unfold. A DH 110 twin-tailed aircraft with swept wings, flown by the De Haviland test pilot John Derry, dived from 40,000 feet towards the airfield, its sonic booms sounding like rumbling gunfire. The plane swept low over the aerodrome, ready to give a display.

Suddenly, without warning, the aircraft broke up. Its cockpit crashed on to the runway and the two engines hurtled towards the ground. The final tally was to be the death of Derry, his Flight Test Observer, and 27 spectators. Another 63 spectators were injured.

Then everyone's eyes were once more directed towards the sky. There, as the crowd stood in stunned silence, a sleek, graceful Hawker Hunter took off. It was being flown by Hawker's chief test pilot, Neville Duke. The crowd was hushed, praying for the lone pilot's safe return. The plane dived, reproducing the sonic booms heard a few minutes before, then carried out a perfect exhibition. Everyone knew that this plane too could break up. It was hard to imagine anyone not marveling at the pilot's courage and ice-cold nerve.

The news was soon out and the world was hearing and reading about the tragedy and Duke's brave flight. Among the many messages that Duke received was one from the Prime Minister, Sir Winston Churchill. It read: 'My Dear Duke, it was characteristic of you and of 615 Squadron to go up yesterday after the shocking accident. Accept my salute'.

The next day, before the cause of the tragedy was yet known, Duke again took up the Hunter, created sonic booms and performed aerial acrobatics in the same patch of sky that he had challenged yesterday. The same place from where John Derry's plane had crashed so fatally.

Neville Frederick Duke was born on January 11th 1922, in Hadlow Road, Tonbridge, Kent. His father, he described as a 'Kentish Man'. As a child, he was always keen on flying and aeromodelling. From his garden, he used to watch the overhead flights to Croydon airfield or headed for Paris and the continent. In time, he learned to spot an Argosy, a Scylla or perhaps a German Junker. The walls of his bedroom were covered with pictures of aircraft and he assembled dozens of models and even a complete airfield, precisely to scale.

He was educated at the local grammar, the Judd School, which he thoroughly enjoyed. He saved every penny of his pocket money and all that he earned from odd jobs to buy a five-shillings (25p) joy ride on a small aircraft from a field near his home. After his first flight, he was quite ecstatic. Then, miracle of miracles, a middle-aged lady asked the young Neville is he would join her in a flight; she didn't want to fly alone. He couldn't believe his good fortune - two flights in one afternoon! After that, he would ride his bicycle far and wide to locate where the next plane rides were being held.

His ambition to fly never wavered. He left school in 1939, shortly before the outbreak of the Second World War. Filling in time before he was old enough at 18 to join up, he worked for six months for an auctioneer and estate agent. He was then turned down for the Fleet Air Arm but in June 1940, accepted by the RAF to train as a pilot.

He was commissioned in February 1941 and operated over France in Spitfires from Biggin Hill. What was it like facing the enemy for the first time? Here is a brief extract from Duke's diary, written after his first action. 'I don't think there is any feeling of fear', he wrote. 'Just an excited urge with a queer feeling inside.'

After a lot more flying, in October 1941, he was posted to the Middle East, to Cairo. On November 30th, he was shot down by a German plane but managed to get out of his Tomahawk and after walking for some time across the desert, was picked up by a British truck, then flown back to base in a Lysander.

Duke's own tally of enemy aircraft shot down was rising and by the end of February 1942 he had been involved in eight confirmed and three probable kills in both the UK and North Africa. In March, he was awarded the Distinguished Flying Cross and completed his first tour the

Neville Frederick Duke, at the controls

following month. This was followed by a rest period of six months, which he spent as an instructor in the Suez Canal zone.

He was promoted to squadron leader and in March 1944 he commenced his third tour as commanding officer in Italy. With this unit he claimed five further kills in May, receiving a second bar to his DFC.

On June 7th, his plane was hit by flak over Lake Bracciano. He tried to bale out and at first found it difficult to get free from the plane. He finally managed this but after hitting the surface of the lake, he was initially held by his parachute and nearly drowned. To make matters worse, he was now behind enemy lines. But Duke's luck held again. Italian partisans looked after him for a while, then smuggled him across the front line and returned him to the allied side. The lake was later referred to by his squadron as 'Duke's Folly'.

After not seeing enemy aircraft for some time, he made his final kills on September 7th 1944. He was now the Mediterranean area's top scorer and by the time his tour of duty had been completed, he had undertaken 486 sorties totalling 712 hours in three tours. He had destroyed 28 enemy aircraft, three probably destroyed and five damaged. At the end of October, he returned to the UK, and arrived home to Tonbridge in the middle of the night - to find the dust sheet still covering his model aerodrome.

Wondering what the Air Ministry planned to do with him, Duke asked for a job that wasn't 'chairbound'. To his delight, on an arrangement with the RAF, he was offered the post of test pilot with Hawker Aircraft in January 1945. He received a quick lesson about how things worked outside the RAF. 'Remember,' he was told, 'the people here are not in uniform. You'll get the best results not by giving orders but by working in with them.'

After a year there, he attended the fourth course at the Empire Test Pilots' School, Cranfield. An outstanding pupil, he was picked for the new High Speed Flight. This was being formed ostensibly to develop the Meteor 4 but mainly to raise the world speed record. This then stood at 606 mph.

Duke now had a number of medals. In 1946, he flew the new Meteor plane to Prague, where he was given a rapturous reception and awarded the Czech War Cross. In 1948 he was given the Air Force Cross. He also set up new point-to-point speed records between London and Rome and London and Karachi. In 1950, he established a new record between London and Cairo.

But there was also time for other things. He met and fell in love with an attractive, dark haired girl named Gwendoline Fellows, from Windsor. They got married on March 15th 1947.

About this time, Duke agonised over whether or not to stay in the RAF. His criteria had always been the same: who would provide him with the most flying? Whatever his experience, whatever his age, the urge to fly remained with him as his greatest passion. He reasoned that the higher your rank in the RAF, the less flying you'd do - and finally decided to go into the commercial field.

So in June 1948, he resigned from the RAF altogether and joined Hawker Aircraft in a permanent post as a test pilot; he was promoted to chief test pilot in April 1951. At the same time, he joined the Royal Auxiliary Air Force. Having flown all the early Hawker jets, he was particularly associated with testing the Hunter, and was awarded the OBE in January 1953.

In early September 1953, one of Hawker's Hunters was made ready to attempt the world speed record. This was then held by the Americans at 715.75 mph. On September 7th, Duke took an all red Hunter up to a speed of 727.63 - a new world record.

In August 1955, he crash landed a Hunter at Thorney Island after the plane had developed a gun-firing problem and injured his back. On May 9th 1956, he sustained further severe injuries after a hard landing and was obliged to resign his position in October 1956. He had received the Queen's Commendation for Valuable Service in the air in 1955.

In the winter of 1959-1960, he grappled with a correspondence course for a full pilot's licence and civil instrument rating, in order to take up a part-time appointment with Sir George Dowty, as his personal pilot. (The Dowty group was a major supplier of components for air forces and aviation world-wide). As well as freelance flying, Duke also carried out consultancy work. In 1960, he formed Duke Aviation Ltd which he managed until 1982 when it was sold.

Throughout his active life, flying had always come first. He would sacrifice most things for this goal. Towards the end of his highly enjoyable autobiography, *Test Pilot*, he sets out what in a sense was his raison d'être: 'I think they (would-be test pilots) will find the work sufficient reward in itself and achieve a tremendous sense of satisfaction and pride in taking part in a job which, I feel, has no equal in any other walk of life in its opportunities for initiative, skill and technical achievement.'

✳   ✳   ✳

The Day of the Eagle

JOSEPHINE MAUD GWYNNE FAIRCLOUGH, MM (1919-)

It was Hermann Goering's term, the Day of the Eagle - August 13, 1940. It was the day during the Battle of Britain that Nazi Germany was going to change the course of the war. But despite the Luffwaiffe's 1,484 blistering sorties, Britain remained undefeated. The RAF claimed the destruction of a staggering 64 German planes. Eagle Day was also the day that the war smashed into Detling and a Kentish girl called Josie Robins entered the history books.

Josie Fairclough (née Robins) in uniform, 1940

There was no inkling of the terror about to be unleashed.

Everyone was becoming used to the series of national warnings given on the telephone and designated by colour. Yellow indicated that the enemy were approximately 22 minutes flying time away and red gave warning of only 12 minutes. Then there was the green message saying that the enemy had gone away and white, when all precautions could be relaxed. Finally, as a kind of fail-safe measure, it had been arranged that the local Observer Corps would telephone Detling airfield when enemy aircraft were approaching.

But no warnings were received that day. Not until the enemy were actually diving over the airfield was the red warning sounded. And by that time it was too late.

It was 4pm and the first sitting for tea were just leaving the mess. The air force men and women heard the howl of the German Stukas above, already diving towards them. And still no siren sounded - just a shout of 'take cover!' and everyone rushed to the nearest dug-out.

The first bomb hit one of the hangers and in a flash, the hanger simply ceased to be. In a series of terrible explosions, the air was suddenly filled with the chaos of war - smoke, flames, rubble and screams.

Corporal Josie Robins had been in the parachute packing section when the attack began. She heard the howl of the engines and saw the German crosses on the planes. She grabbed her tin hat and rushed outside. It was bedlam. People were tearing about everywhere. Where the hanger used to be, there was now a raging fire. The nearest shelter wasn't far from the mess and she managed to push her way inside.

The atmosphere inside the shelter was claustrophobic and the noise deafening. There was the sound of WAAFs crying and of airmen saying their last prayers. Everyone realised that death could be very near.

Then a bomb landed just beside them. The shelter shook and much of the roof fell on the occupants. The dust and fumes choked them. Chalk and stones fell on top of them. The end of the shelter furthest away from Josie seemed to be worst hit; there were many calls of distress. Getting up from the floor, she peered out. The German planes had gone and everywhere there was a strange silence as if the world was waiting for something more to happen.

Checking if any of her bones were broken, she found only a few cuts and bruises. Slowly the men and women from the shelter began to emerge. Many started to clear the rubble with their bare hands and to help the wounded. Josie went to the far end of the shelter, where the worst of the wounded seemed to be. It was very dark and she realised that the roof might collapse at any moment. Despite this, she administered first aid, staying there for some time, doing what was necessary. When she had done all she could, she helped in removing the dead. The raid had killed several men and two were seriously injured.

Emerging into the daylight again, she was confronted by the WAAF Commanding Officer, Miss Cope, who demanded to know where Josie had been!

Josie Maud Gwynne Robins was born on February 5th, 1919. Before the war, she gave riding lessons in Faversham. When hostilities seemed imminent, she joined the 19th Company WAAF, at Astley House in Maidstone, where she became part of the catering unit. She was given training and attended lectures in the evenings and sometimes at weekends. In August 1939, the auxiliaries were incorporated fully into the RAF and she was sent to Detling airfield, high on the North Downs, between Maidstone and Sittingbourne.

Detling was a Coastal Command airfield under the control of No 16 (General Reconnaissance) Group with its headquarters at nearby

Chatham. The resident squadron at this time was No 500 (County of Kent) of the Royal Auxiliary Air Force, which had moved to the airfield from Manston in 1938.

Josie came from a military family; her father had been a cavalry captain in the First World War and now became a home guard. Josie's mother joined the Women's Voluntary Service.

Detling was a busy airfield with its Ansons engaged in bombing enemy ports in France and Hollland and on escort duties for shipping through the Channel. All this meant long hours for Josie, feeding both air-crew and ground-crew.

At first, her CO, Miss Cope, was the only woman given a uniform (and a khaki one at that). The likes of Josie had only an armband to distinguish them. In the freezing winter of 1939/40, however, the Air Ministry issued an airman's greatcoat to all the serving women. And eventually everyone received a proper WAAF uniform.

Their living quarters gave few of life's comforts. The WAAFs were billeted in cottages close to the airfield boundary. Their only form of heating was a central coal fire and in winter the pipes froze.

In the aftermath of Eagle Day, when much of Detling was destroyed, Josie's catering unit had to manage on a large cooking stove fuelled by petrol. With many of the billets gone, private houses in the area had to be requisitioned. A makeshift operations room was organised.

Josie went on a short leave, when the Air Ministry phoned her mother to say that she had been awarded the Military Medal for bravery. At first, Josie thought her mother was joking. She received her medal from the King at Buckingham Palace in the spring of 1941. According to the citation, she had 'shown courage and coolness of a very high order in a position of extreme danger.'

But further honours were to come her way. Josie's portrait was commissioned by the Air Ministry, which meant her sitting for three weeks in Malvern for the distinguished painter, Dame Laura Knight. Josie was also promoted to Warrant Officer.

In 1944, she married James Fairclough, an RAF transport sergeant she met at Detling. When peace returned, they went into farming at Sandway, Kent, where they are today.

In May 1989, Josie and James were invited to the old Duxford Officers' mess to see her portrait once again. Today, Josie often visits the places where the bombs fell; for the Kent County Show is now held on part of what was the old Detling airfield. And here Josie has her memories...

✳   ✳   ✳

Kent Firemen. Heroes every one.

Kent firemen risk their lives almost every time they respond to an emergency call. And this applies as much to the 'retained' (on call) firemen as to the staff members. Come a disaster like a major blaze or even an old lady's favourite pet cat trapped up a tree - and out of the blue come the firemen asking for nothing but to serve. Over the years, many have been injured, some killed.

FEARLESS WORK DURING ENEMY ACTION

The Second World War wasn't quite a year old on July 29th 1940. Dover Harbour suffered a large-scale attack by enemy bombers. Fires were started on ships and oil stores. Air raids continued throughout the day. During the day, all members of the Dover Fire Brigade and the Auxiliary Fire Service engaged in the fire fighting did excellent work in difficult and dangerous circumstances and the fires were eventually extinguished.

Deputy Fire Chief CWA Brown, Executive Officer E Harmer and Section Officer A Campbell worked aboard HMS *Sandhurst,* where torpedoes, ammunition, and spilled fuel oil threatened to explode at any minute. The three Dover men were awarded the George Cross, in the first

Deputy Fire Chief, CWA Brown; Executive Officer E Harmer and Section Officer A Campbell.

list of awards of the new medal.

A number of others received Commendations from the King. These were The Dover Fire Brigade, the Dover Auxiliary Fire Service, Fireman Ernest Alfred Foord (Dover Fire Brigade), Fireman Edward Jesse Gore (Dover Fire Brigade), Station Officer Harold Thomas Hookings (Dover Fire Brigade), Auxiliary Fireman Arthur Thomas Cunnington (AFS), Auxiliary Fireman Rupert Hudsmith (AFS), and Auxiliary Fireman John McDermott (AFS). On Monday September 30th, 1940 the Mayor handed them the official record of the deed and congratulated them in the name of Dover.

AMIDST EXPLODING SHELLS AND EXPLOSIVES

It was September 10th 1940 and a fire was raging in the Woolwich Arsenal. Shells were exploding and flying debris seemed to be everywhere. The four adjacent buildings all contained large quantities of explosives. Two men, Margate journalist and auxiliary fireman, Henry Harrison Stephen Kinlan, and another man by the name of Storer, assisted in saving the buildings. Both remained at their posts despite being reminded of the immanent danger of explosion. Both men were awarded the George Medal. Little was reported about Storer but it is known Harry Kinlan attended Margate Central School before going straight into journalism on a local newspaper. After the war, he turned down a lucrative offer to become fire officer for a major car firm and returned to his first love, journalism. He worked on papers in Margate, Canterbury and Woolwich, then moved to Fleet Street with Extel. Kinlan is believed to be the first journalist to be awarded the George Cross.

FIVE HOURS FOR LIFE

In March 1942, at Dover, a woman was trapped under a bombed house. Second Lieutenant JLG Warren of the Buffs Regiments saw what had happened and tunnelled under the debris for about 100 feet. A lot of timber and debris lay on the woman, which Warren managed to ease off her with the aid of two small jacks. Despite the realisation that the rest of the house might crash on top of them at any moment, the Lieutenant stayed with the woman for five hours, continuing to give her encouraging words and keeping her face clear of dust and debris. On the instructions of a doctor, he gave her morphine injections twice.

Warren's courage undoubtedly saved the woman's life, for which he was awarded the George Medal. It was announced in the *London Gazette* on September 18th 1942.

GHOST HUNTING ENDS IN TRAGEDY

On January 27th 1962, two lads set out to 'lay a ghost' in the 11th century ruined mansion, Oxney Court, St Margaret's. While attempting to lift a heavy door off the ground, one of them slipped and fell into a 180-feet well. The other boy went for help. The Dover brigade responded, arriving at 10.54am. Leading Fireman A Young was lowered by a line to recover the injured boy, who was found to be dead on arrival at the hospital.

For carrying out this hazardous rescue, Mr. Young was awarded the Chief Officer's Commendation Certificate.

100 FEET DOWN

On April 6th 1965, at 9.15pm, the Medway fire brigade was called to Street Farm, Burham, to rescue a man who had fallen 140 feet down the working shaft of a disused quarry. A seven-foot high wire mesh fence and barbed wire surrounded the shaft; and this had to be cut before a rescue was attempted.

Fireman J A Brain, with a signalling line, torch and wearing breathing apparatus, was let down on a 120-foot rescue line, to which another had been attached. A Neil-Robertson stretcher (a special kind of stretcher made of canvas and slats of wood which wraps around the body) was also lowered - to which the injured man was fastened. Brain and the stretcher were then hauled to the surface together. Brain managed to protect the injured man from contact with the sides of the shaft and from falling earth and chalk.

The rescued man had fractured both feet and his back, and had lacerations and a suspected fracture of the jaw. Because of the man's extreme pain, he could not himself offer any assistance in his own rescue. This made it far more difficult for Brain to put him into the stretcher.

Fireman J A Brain was awarded a Commendation Certificate. The Queen gave orders that his name was to appear in a supplement to the *London Gazette* on August 10th 1965.

RESCUE FROM THE BOTTOM OF A WELL

At 8.04pm on August 22nd 1965, an alarm call went out that a boy had fallen down a well. Two fire engines heard the call and both responded.

The well was approximately 325 feet in depth, brick lined, with a diameter at the top of three feet, reducing to two-feet, six-inches at the bottom. The floor of the well was covered with debris, including corrugated iron sheeting, roof timbers and steel girders. And from that distance down, there was no way of knowing if the boy was alive or dead.

Special cliff rescue apparatus was ordered from Folkestone and a test made with lamps to determine the condition of the air in the well. It was found to be unbreathable below 150 feet.

Fireman B J Shoveller, from Sittingbourne Fire Station, was lowered by the cliff rescue apparatus, together with a Neil-Robertson stretcher. On reaching the bottom, he found the body of the boy, badly mutilated and entangled in the debris. It was not possible to put the body onto the stretcher so with great difficulty he managed to secure it to a line. This could then be hauled up from the top. Again with much difficulty, the boy's body and Fireman Shoveller were brought to the surface.

The time taken had been 55 minutes and just as he reached the top, Shoveller's breathing apparatus whistle sounded: he had barely enough oxygen to last for another five minutes.

Fireman B J Shoveller was congratulated and awarded first a Commendation Certificate and later the British Empire Medal (Civil Division). The notice appeared in a Supplement to the *London Gazette* on December 21st 1965.

All other members of the brigade who took part in the rescue received official congratulations.

THE DAY THE EARTH OPENED

Just after three o'clock in the afternoon on November 21st 1967, a woman was walking near her home, 125 Cooling Road, Strood, when the ground simply opened up and she fell down a hole 100-feet deep. The opening at ground level was quite small but it widened in places to 25-feet or more. At the bottom it converged to become an opening of about eight feet across. Below that it simply ended in an old flooded culvert.

The fire brigade responded quickly to a call and an officer and two firemen were lowered into the hole. The women's body, however, had been washed away in the culvert and was never recovered. The two firemen were injured by falling debris.

For outstanding courage in attempting the rescue, Officer J Lipscombe and Firemen H Myers and R F Boulstridge were awarded Commendation Certificates.

DOVER'S WORST DISASTER SINCE THE WAR

To the firemen who went on duty at six o'clock on Saturday March 26th 1977, it was just another routine night. They had the occasional visitor, some played table tennis, others watched an indifferent Match of the Day on television, still others slept or read.

Then just before 3am, the alert signal came rudely over the loudspeaker, shattering their peace. As one man, they sprung to. As usual, they were soon ready and within minutes, were on their way to a fire at the Crypt Restaurant. They didn't know it then but it was to be the worst fire Dover had had in over 20 years. And not all of the firemen who attended this fire would be coming back.

As this was happening, Station Officer Anthony Peters was receiving a similar alarm call at his home and retained firemen in homes all around Dover were being roused by their personal bleepers. The fire was a big one and involved not only the Crypt Restaurant, but also the popular Shakespeare bars and flats in Bench street. A large turnout was needed and in the end more than 100 rescuers were involved.

Ladywell Road came alive in seconds. Dave Dadd, Jim Hogben, Ken ('Taff') Fairchild, Nigel Baker, Bill Price and Bobby Greenfield were quickly in position on the water tender ladder. And John Walton and Graham Gash were soon heading for the fire on the 100-foot turntable ladder.

Price, the former Dover goalkeeper, and Baker, manned a ladder to the front of the building to rescue people trapped above the restaurant. Hogben and Fairchild, both wearing breathing apparatus, went into the smoke-filled building to try and find other occupants known to be on the premises.

Meanwhile, Walton and Gash were using their giant ladder to rescue people on the roof. The only man not immediately visible in the dark and smoke was Greenfield who was manning pumps - maintaining the supply of water being pumped onto the fire.

Within 14 minutes of receiving the alarm call the team had rescued 13 people from the building. Six died. And as the debris fell down all around him, John English, photographer with the Dover Express, described it as one of his most spectacular assignments. That was the word of a hardened press photographer. But hardened as he was, he confessed that one of his worst moments came when a fireman brought out the body of a dead child in his arms.

The alert had begun at 2.49am. Former police officer Peter Waters, of Dolphin House, Dover, had been watching television. He started to take his dog for a walk when - in his own words - 'I saw smoke coming from under the doors of the restaurant on the ground floor. I dashed to the Market Square and phoned the fire brigade. They were on the spot quickly.'

At one stage, several Folkestone firemen were trapped by a girder on the ground floor of the restaurant. Dover firemen fought with their bare hands to release them. Soon there were a dozen firemen to the rescue. Two of the trapped men were rescued practically unhurt and two more could be seen partially covered by the floor that had fallen from above.

'One of the rescuers said later: 'we dug until they brought a chain saw to cut through the wood. One of those we brought out was conscious, the other unconscious.

'We were told Leading Fireman Sharp was still missing. We found him in the same area covered by a girder and by pieces from the floor above. We worked hard to move the debris but he was dead when we got him out' said a fireman.

Some of the Folkestone firemen were taken to Canterbury Hospital. David Waters was suffering from burns to his right side and injuries to his chest, and James Wright had a back injury. Retained Fireman Albert James, from Hythe, sustained an injured ankle.

This Dover fire had been a big one. But every week, Kent firemen are attending to other emergencies, great and small. And when they do, they carry out the work with the same courage and coolness that they showed so well in Dover on Saturday March 26th 1977.

Red Cross and St John's Ambulance Pioneer

John Furley (1836-1919)

John Furley spent a lifetime proving his parents wrong. In the days of strict parental control, he was made to bow to their conviction that he was 'not strong enough for the Army' - a passion he had had since childhood. Instead - throughout his lifetime - he was to repeatedly face the horrors of war at close quarters and devoted his time to the relief of the suffering of war.

It is hard to think of any other Kent hero who has done more - in the motto of Furley's own St John's Ambulance - 'for the service of mankind'.

John Furley was born in North Street, Ashford (where a commemorative bronze plaque marks what is now The Masonic Hall) on March 19th 1836. He was the son of Robert Furley, solicitor, JP, and antiquarian, and his wife, Margaret. That his father should have denied him a military career must have been particularly harsh, as the army seems to have always been in the young lad's

Sir John Furley disguised as a coachman

blood. He spent most of his early school holidays strutting around the barrack square at Maidstone, with the connivance of two of his father's friends - the Generals Middleton and Griffiths.

John was educated at Harrow and when leaving, given the choice of either going up to university or touring abroad with a tutor. He chose the latter, later admitting that this gave him a far better opportunity 'to see more of military life than was compatible with civil studies'.

John's health had always proved unpredictable and he was twice rejected in his attempts to join the Army to see action in the Crimea. He even tried going to the war as an observer but found this wasn't possible. Nothing daunted, off his own bat, he travelled to Copenhagen to observe Denmark's resistance against the armies of Prussia and Austria. He even insisted he be allowed to spend time with the soldiers under canvas.

Returning home to England, he gave in to family pressures to take up law. He put in a number of hours studying in the Temple but his heart simply wasn't in it. He preferred instead his daily visit to the Albany Street barracks where he drilled with the Scots Guards. He did, however, work for a time in his father's solicitor's office in Ashford (the firm became known as Hallett, Creery & Furley, and later as Hallett & Co.)

Still having a burning desire to be in the armed forces, he joined the 29th Kent (Ashford) Volunteers, in which he was eventually promoted to captain. John accompanied the Volunteers on visits to the Continent. Here he met the King of the Netherlands, the King of the Belgiums, the King of Prussia, and was seen at the best social occasions. He even smoked a cigar with Bismark.

Taking up the altruism of his father, (if not his enthusiasm for the law) John was much concerned by the suffering of war wounded. He took a great interest in the Order of St John and was received as a member of the 'Sovereign and Illustrious Order of St John of Jerusalem: Anglia'. He was later made a Knight of Justice of the Order.

Furley sat on the committee, which pledged Britain's support for the formation of the Red Cross. First steps were taken at the historic Geneva conference of 1864. In the following year the Red Cross convention was ratified by all the great powers. The symbol of a red cross against a white background was approved and it was agreed that military hospitals, the wounded, and Red Cross personnel were to be acknowledged as neutral and non-combatants. The first test for the new society came on July 15th with the start of the Franco-Prussian War.

Furley later described what happened next as 'one of the most important chapters of my life'. After he had approached a number of contacts, the British National Society for the Sick and Wounded was formed; it included a good many members of the Order of St John. Furley and a Dr McCormac were put in charge of the Anglo-American Ambulance Unit to go to the war zone.

Although he had steeled himself to work under the conditions of war, Furley never lost his compassion for the suffering. At Gravelotte, he saw roofless cottages, crammed to overflowing with wounded men. 'Imagine,' he told friends, 'a vast plain terminating towards the horizon in verdant woods and pastures; in the midst a heap of blackened ruins; gardens trodden down, trees torn with shot; all around bursting graves, refuse of bivouacs, dead horses, broken tumbrils, arms, empty ammunition barrels.'

He became separated from his own ambulance unit but set up an improvised ambulance group in Belgium. They appropriated a house in Douzy, near Sedan, as a store for food, drink, and medicines. A small hospital was set up in a deserted cafe, where Furley took his share of the many menial tasks. They had their difficulties with marauders and Furley captured one bandit personally. He reported the matter to a German officer who then gave orders for the thief to be 'shooted'. Disagreeing with this drastic sentence, Furley let the prisoner slip away. It proved a fruitless gesture - the man died of smallpox within the week.

At the Caserne d'Asfeld, Furley had a grand reunion with the Anglo-American ambulance. But after making sure the Sedan hospitals were well equipped, he decided to move on. Paris was now under siege by the Germans. Furley nevertheless planned to get into the city, where he felt he might be able to do some good. After an incident in which he was nearly shot as a spy, he accepted the disappointing news that he would not be allowed to enter Paris. He thus made his way to Versailles, where he remained for five months, until the Armistice. He tried to divide his time evenly between the French and the German sick and wounded.

He travelled to Beaugency, from where he wrote: 'I have seen death in many places, but seldom have I seen him stalking about so rapidly as here ...'

Sydney Hall, illustrator with the *Graphic,* was so appalled that he left the scene and went off to sketch the near-by peaceful river. Furley brought him back and forced him to depict the full horrors of war he saw there with his own eyes.

The Beaugency Theatre was crowded with the dead and the still living - 'the squalor, misery and hopelessness were utterly appalling.' The remnants of the last theatrical performance still lay grotesquely about on the stage. The artist forced himself to sketch what he saw; it later appeared in the Graphic under the caption 'Theatre de la Guerre'.

Furley returned to Versailles, more than ever determined to see Paris for himself. Meeting nothing but refusals at official level, he thought up a ruse to get him through the check posts. Furley became a full liveried coachman, splendid in his uniform. He was stopped by both German and French troops, but at last managed to get inside the city. He immediately made himself known to the headquarters of the French Red Cross, at Rue Lafitte, where he was well received.

Realising the need for fresh food, he returned to Versailles and the next day - well provisioned - set off again for Paris. He travelled unmolested, drawing the comment from one post that he took as a compliment: 'It is only M Furley who goes everywhere without a pass'.

The British embassy spoke in a similar vein. He was given a room at the embassy to use as a depot. Furley moved about, apparently leading a charmed life, sailing unscathed through all incidents. This caused one of the diplomats to say that: 'The embassy would spare itself any further anxiety on his behalf, since he was plainly able to take care of himself'.

In an attempt to help the farmers produce more food, Furley accepted the chairmanship of the Paris branch of the Peasant Farmers' Seed Fund.

Revolutionaries now plunged Paris into a state of terror. During March, April and May, civil order broke down. Through the ensuing melee, Furley worked on. His position in the seed fund brought him unexpected luck as his picture appeared in all the huge posters, which now littered the city. But when the season had so advanced that it was no longer possible to plant the seed, he went back to his ambulance and welfare work.

At last the government began to regain control. On Good Friday, Versailles troops stormed the Bridge of Neuilly. Furley and his friends were there to attend to the wounded.

He was appalled by the state of things; everywhere there were huge piles of uncollected rubbish. Then the communists set fire to the city, hostages were murdered and Furley was sickened by the needless waste of human life. The bodies of 5,000 communists lay in long parallel trenches. On May 31st, Marshal McMohon issued the final proclamation: 'A week of horror, unparalleled in the history of the world is over'.

In 1875, Furley enjoyed a brief respite from war when he attended the wedding in St Petersburg of the Duke of Edinburgh and the Russian princess, Marie. To defray expenses, Furley managed to get himself employed by the Standard. The marriage was well written up; Furley then moved on to Moscow for the reception of the Imperial Family.

He returned home but had hardly done more than set foot in England before he was once more needed in another theatre of war - this time the Carlist War in Spain. For a man so opposed to the carnage of war, he was also capable of total objectivity. He described the battle of Estella as the 'grandest and most picturesque I had ever witnessed'.

He now became involved in the rescue of a young British special correspondent named O'Donovan. It was thought that the young man was held inside a Carlist jail. Following a series of clues, Furley approached the influential Dona Margarita, wife of Don Carlos. At first, she said firmly that the matter 'had better be forgotten'. But after a lengthy argument, Furley managed to convince her of O'Donovan's innocence - that he was certainly no spy. With the help of Dona Margarita, he had at last managed to track down the young Irishman who he found in a pitiful state. He managed to prise O'Donovan from his captors and - after a hazardous journey - saw the correspondent over the Spanish border.

Returning to England in November 1874, Furley married a girl call Maria. In his autobiographical *In Peace and War,* he calls the wedding 'the most important event in my life'. Despite this he devotes barely a paragraph to his wife. We learn that she was sympathetic to his beliefs, and never failed to give him encouragement and practical support.

Furley enjoyed the company of his friends in the Order of St John. There was much concern about the number of accidents produced by a thriving industrial society. A seminal paper was drafted by Sir Thomas Longmore: 'The preliminary care and attention necessary for accidental bodily injuries where many workpeople are employed'. For the first time, broad lines were publicly discussed and laid down by experts as 'First Aid to the Injured'.

In August 1877, Furley was asked by the Financial Secretary to the War Office to go to Montenegro. He was to report on the state of the wounded soldiers and the conditions of the hospitals there. He travelled via Paris, Turin and Venice, then by boat down the Adriatic, disembarked at Bocche de Cattaro and continued on horseback. The capital, a single-street community, reminded Furley of one of the more primitive Irish villages. He was looked after by the Russian Red Cross and found the wounded to be well cared for in simple buildings or under canvas.

At the beginning of 1899 Furley was knighted by the Queen - 'after 40 years' labour as Commissioner for the Sick and Wounded Soldiers and service during five campaigns of War'.

In the same year, an official link was made between the existing volunteer groups and the War Office. The Central British Red Cross Committee had only been formed the previous summer. It comprised the Army Nursing Reserve, the National Aid Society (known as the English or British Red Cross Society) and the St John Ambulance Association. Furley acted as treasurer.

In the autumn of that year, the new body faced its first challenge: war broke out in South Africa. Sir John was asked to design and command a hospital train, to equip it fully and send it out to South Africa. It was a tall order but he felt quite up to the job. For years - since about 1870 - he had been taking notes of trains throughout his travels. The new train was completed in ten weeks, a fortnight ahead of schedule.

Lady Furley accompanied her husband to South Africa and the first journey was to Ladysmith. The new train then returned to Durban with ten officers and 54 men, who could not otherwise have been moved. They were all safely placed on board a hospital ship. During the 18 months of Sir John's control, the train made 108 journeys and covered 42,115 miles. Of the 7,429 patients carried, there were only six deaths.

In the First World War, despite his advanced age, Sir John was able to do more than his bit for the Red Cross. The original 25 huts, the nucleus of the great base hospital at Netley, were designed under his personal supervision and these served as a model for later additions. He also devoted all his skill and experience to the designing of hospital trains for use at the front and their efficiency was in no small degree due to him.

When what he wanted wasn't available, he invented it. At first he gave the designs to practical experts but later decided that it was easiest to make up the items himself. Some were modest affairs like the small ambulance hamper, complete with waterproof cover and fitted with splints, bandages and other items. Other inventions were larger, like litters, stretchers, and ambulance carriages. He invented a two-wheeled litter, combining a stretcher with an undercarriage.

He set up a manufacturing base in Ashford at Marshall's Carriage Works in New Street. Before the end of the century, this had produced 6,000 stretchers and litters, and 100 horse ambulance carriages.

A year or so before Sir John's death, he was burgled and all his decorations stolen. The thief got quite a haul. In his long heroic career, Sir John Furley received many marks of public recognition, addresses, medals and decorations. Besides his knighthood, he was a Companion of Honour, a Knight of Justice and Honorary Bailiff of the Order of St John; he was also given the South African War Medal. In addition to these, he had an impressive number of awards and decorations from many overseas countries.

Not at all bad for a man considered unfit for action.

God's Englishman

CHARLES GEORGE GORDON (1833-1885)

On the morning of January 28th, 1885, when the advance party of the British force sent to relieve the siege at Khartoum discovered they were two days too late and that Gordon had been murdered, the native soldiers threw themselves down and wept. 'We have lost our families', they cried, 'our properties and everything belonging to us, that is the fortune of war: but Gordon is dead, by the will of God, all is finished.'

A week later, at Korti, 280 miles from Khartoum, at 7 pm on February 4th, General Lord Wolesley, commander of the relieving force, heard the news as he was going into dinner. 'I shall never see his like again', he wrote...'many generations may come and go without producing a Charlie Gordon...as long as we continue to be manly enough to revere the highest form of courage and devotion, so long will [Gordon] be quoted and referred to...I never knew but two heroes...[Gordon] was one'. (He didn't say who the other was).

At Osborne House in the Isle of Wight, Queen Victoria was shocked by 'the dreadful news...' She wrote, 'The Govt is alone to blame, by refusing to send an expedition till it was too late...'

In the same year as his death, Gordon's niece wrote: 'everyone who ever saw Uncle Charlie loved him and when he talked to you, you could feel how much he loved God and was looking out for an opportunity to serve Him.'

And in Gravesend, in Kent, there was an extra special reason for mourning. For it was here that Gordon spent the most peaceful and happiest time of his life. It was here that he taught in his Ragged School and promoted the street urchins to be his adopted 'kings' - giving them a new start in life and a secure job in Her Majesty's ships.

Who was this man responsible for such a universal outpouring of grief? For he was mourned not only in England but in Europe also and across the civilised world. It was the common belief that a warrior-saint had been martyred.

Charles George Gordon was born fourth son of Lieutenant-General Henry William Gordon, Royal Artillery and Elizabeth, daughter of Samuel Enderby of Croom's Hill, Blackheath. He went to school in Taunton in 1843 and entered the Royal Military Academy at Woolwich in 1848.

An example of his attitude to the rigours of the world is seen early in his years at the Academy. One morning in the beginning of winter, it was announced on the parade ground that doctor's orders were that the cadets were not to use the open-air swimming pool on the common. Gordon, with his slight lisp muttered: 'Damn nonthence, coddling young soldiers. Let's bath all winter and prove it's wholesome and the doctor a fool.' After that, the cadets did indeed follow Gordon's advice, even though they sometimes had to break the ice.

Portrait of Gordon in Mandarin costume by Val Prinsep, 1867.

Gordon was commissioned a second lieutenant in the Royal Engineers on June 23rd 1852, aged 19. In the Crimean War (1853-1856), he distinguished himself by his reckless bravery in the trenches outside Sevastopol. Garnet Wolseley, the future field-marshal commented on Gordon's 'indifference to danger of all sorts, or I should rather say, an apparent unconsciousness of it'. Years later, Gordon admitted to a friend that he had gone 'to the Crimea hoping, without having a hand in it, to be killed'. To Gordon, death was at the gate to everlasting life.

He also earned the respect from his fellow officers by his ability to gain useful intelligence on the movements of the enemy. The military historian, Colonel Chesney heard that Gordon developed 'a personal knowledge of the enemy's movements such as no other officer attained. Or put by another observer, 'If you want to know what the Russians are up to, send for Charlie Gordon'.

After the surrender of Sevastopol, he was responsible for the destruction of the enemy's docks there. For his many exploits in the Crimea, he was awarded the British war medal and clasp, the Turkish war medal, and the French Legion of Honour.

From the spring to the autumn of 1858, Gordon was employed in a frontier delimitation survey in Bessarabia, Kurdistan and Armenia. He camped amongst wild tribesmen and although only 24, found himself the sole authority keeping the peace between Russians and Turks.

While still in his twenties, Gordon made a note in his diary that he somehow had a mission to fulfil and that he would carry this out unmarried. His call, he believed, would not come in the conventional life of the barracks or in court society but in the dangerous and unknown places of the world.

On April 1st 1859, he was promoted Captain and his future destiny began to take shape. In the following year he volunteered to join the British and French forces, operating against China. He was present at the capture of Peking in October 1860 and personally directed the burning of the emperor's summer palace. For his services in this campaign, he was rewarded with the British war medal with clasp.

In May 1862, Gordon's corps of engineers strengthened the bulwarks of the European Trading Centre in Shanghai, which was threatened by insurgents of the Taiping Rebellion.

A year later, he took command of a force of around 3,500 Chinese peasants with European officers - known as the Ever Victorious Army. They had not in the past lived up to their name but under Gordon's command, achieved a string of victories against the rebels. Gordon led his army with no weapon but a wooden cane, christened his magic wand.

He was credited as a man who knew the three secrets of war - when to strike, where to strike and how to strike. In less than three years, after 33 engagements, the power of the Taiping rebels was completely broken.

But everywhere, this incorruptible man was up against the prevailing state of the world as it was. Some of the Europeans serving with Gordon went across to the enemy for higher pay. But even in the face of treachery, Gordon could be magnanimous. One such man was brought to him one day as a wounded prisoner. Loudly Gordon ordered the man to be shot. But he then spoke softly to the escort, 'put him in my boat, let the doctor attend him and send him down to Shanghai'.

Many battles had been won but the war itself was not over. Soo-chow, for centuries known for its wealth, had not yet been taken. But at last the Wangs, the rebel leaders, were willing to accept Gordon's authority if he spared their lives. Gordon agreed to this and made it clear to Governor-general Li. However, as soon as the imperial army marched through the gates, Li order the execution of the Wangs.

Gordon felt this act of treachery very deeply. He resigned his command and when, on January 1st 1864, money and rewards were heaped upon him, he refused them all. The gift of 10,000 taels of silver - a considerable sum - was donated to the British Museum.

In the months following, it became clear that if Gordon did not once again take to the field, the Taipings would regain the territory they had lost. On the urgent representation of the British envoy at Peking, Governor Li was compelled to issue a proclamation exonerating Gordon from all complicity in the murder of the Wangs.

Gordon agreed to once more take charge of the army and some of the most bitter fighting of the campaign took place in which Gordon himself was wounded. In February 1864, he was promoted colonel. By June the rebels were finally dispersed. Gordon's name was riding high and in Europe he was given the name Chinese Gordon. It was even said that Gordon was more powerful than the emperor. He once again refused a large money payment, though he had spent his army pay promoting the efficiency of his force. He wrote home saying, 'I will leave China as poor as when I entered it.'

He did, however, accept the emperor's present of the yellow jacket and peacock's feather of a mandarin of the first class, and a gold medal of distinction. His title was Ti-Tu, the highest military rank in China. The British awarded him the Companion of the Order of the Bath (CB).

Colonel Gordon sailed home from Shanghai on the P & O steamer, *Hyson*. In China, he had been regarded as a saint and a hero. To his own people - because of his general disdain of riches - he was an enigma. But now, in Gravesend, in Kent, the great humanitarian work of his life was about to begin.

In September 1865, he was appointed Royal Engineers Officer in command, to supervise the construction of forts for the defence of the Thames. Gordon considered such a project to be a waste of public money but it was typical of the man that he nevertheless carried out his orders to the letter. The job was not onerous and he found he had plenty of time to carry out his charitable works.

These were mainly concerned with the poor ragged boys, which he found on the streets of Gravesend. He would rescue them, take them into his house and personally bath, feed and clothe them. He set up a ragged school and with the help of an assistant teacher, taught the basics of reading, writing, mathematics, and studies from the Bible. Then, when the boys were ready, he would get them a job, usually as sailors. On a large wall map of the world, he would then follow their positions as they sailed around the globe.

His official residence in Gravesend was Fort House, a former rectory.

Gordon opened the gardens to old people on summer evenings. Then, when one said how pleasant it would be to have a garden of his own, Gordon divided the garden into sections to be used by the local poor for growing vegetables and anything else they fancied.

As the costs for all his charitable work had to come out of his own pocket, he had to scrimp and save to enable him to do what he wanted. The clothing bill for his 'kings' as he called them covered literally hundreds of suits and by the time he left Gravesend, he was buying boots by the gross.

During this period, he developed his own unorthodox, mystical brand of Christianity and distributed thousand of religious tracts he had printed at his own expense.

The 'Kernel' as he was known to his young lads never gave up on a child. Some of the boys he had washed, fed and clothed would run away and Gordon would find them again weeks later, in the back streets, dressed in dirty rags and half-starved. He would then begin the process all over again. Some ran away again several times and each time Gordon would attempt to rescue them.

Despite the run-aways, the boys usually behaved well for Gordon. The story of one boy, Scott, was typical. At the Ragged School, the lad was determined to do all he could to be a disruption. He joined a class that he thought was Gordon's but was really run by the assistant teacher. Scott caused such a commotion that the teacher was forced to take a holiday. During the teacher's absence, Gordon took the class. On the teacher's return, he asked how Scott had got on. Gordon answered truthfully that Scott 'was the best boy in the class'.

It was the same charisma that had compelled the Chinese peasants in the Always Victorious Army to follow Gordon into the heat of the battle. It was the same magnetism that caused men of all nationalities to do what ever Gordon asked of them.

In 1871, Colonel Gordon received an invitation to join the Danubian Commission. This had developed from boundary commissions in the Crimea, on which Gordon had worked before he went to China. In Constantinople he met Nubae Pasha, the foreign minister of Ismail, Khedive of Egypt. The Khedive was accustomed to employing Europeans and offered Gordon the post of Governor of the Equatorial Provinces of the Sudan. Gordon's salary was £10,000 a year, of which he would accept only £2000. Of the remaining 13 years of his life, Gordon was to spend seven in the Sudan.

Gordon reached Khartoum on 13th March 1874 but stayed only a few days. He arrived at Gondokoro, the seat of government, on April 16th. He found the countryside so unsafe that the garrison would not move out of the town except in armed bands. Gordon saw the enormity of the task and met it head on. Within the course of a year, he had gained the confidence of the natives, made the country safe, formed and garrisoned eight stations, enforced the government monopoly on ivory and sent sufficient money to Cairo to pay all the expenses of the expedition.

By the close of the year, eight of the small staff of Europeans had died. He wrote 'no one can conceive the utter misery of these lands. Heat and mosquitoes day and night, all the year round.' He thus transferred the seat of government to the more healthy station of Laido.

From April 1874 to December 1876, he mapped the upper Nile and established a line of stations as far south as present Uganda. He established a chain of forts, a day's journey apart. But - from Gordon's point of view - he had begun an even greater task. From the beginning of time, as far as anybody knew, the area had traded in black and white ivory, the former being the bodies of men, women and children sold into slavery. Gordon managed to make some inroads against slavery but this was opposed by Ismail Pasha Yacaub, the governor-general of the Sudan. Gordon therefore resigned his post at the end of 1876 and returned to England.

As far as Gordon was concerned, that was to be the end of that. But the Khedive, in dire financial straits and surrounded on all sides by corrupt ministers and greedy Europeans, turned to the only man in the world that he could trust. Gordon agreed to return in January 1877. But this time, he set his own terms. He demanded - and got - the position of Governor General of the entire Sudan, an area the size of Europe, excluding Russia. He was to improve communications and - a goal Gordon set for himself - attempt to eradicate the slave trade.

There was no telegraph or railways and Gordon was forced to travel personally vast distances over his domain - so much so that he became a legend in the land. Dressed in the richly embroidered uniform of a Turkish Marshal, the governor general overtook his escorts, dashing solo from one place to another - opening up communications, augmenting his striking force, freeing slaves and drilling them as soldiers, and establishing posts at water holes. He achieved this by marching day and night, through terrifying sand storms and torrential rains, apparently unaffected by the normal pangs of hunger and thirst and the need for sleep. Within four months - with craven troops he hadn't had time to discipline - he had uprooted rebellion and restrained the power of the slave-kings.

But there was little support to be expected from England. Gordon wrote of his exasperation. 'The people of England care more for their dinners than they do for anything else.' Then, in defining the kind of helper he required, he described himself. 'Find me the man who utterly despises name, money, honour and glory; who never wishes to see his home again; who looks to God as the source of good and the controller of evil; one who has a healthy body and energetic spirit and who looks on death as a release from misery'.

Gordon lacked proper backing, both at home and in the Sudan. His proposals for the reorganisation of government finances were met with local rejection. There were too many corrupt officials doing very nicely thank you. It is ironical that about this time Gordon cut his own annual salary from £6000 to £3000.

But his exertions and the awful climate were proving too much even for Gordon's constitution and early in 1880 he went to Switzerland for a complete rest.

After only a few weeks, he received a telegram offering him command of the colonial forces at the Cape of Good Hope, which he declined. A change of government in Britain brought another invitation - that of Secretary to the new Viceroy of India, which he accepted. This was followed by several other positions and during the next two years he served in India, China, South Africa and Mauritius.

In 1884, Gordon was again sent to the Sudan to evacuate Egyptian forces from Khartoum, which was threatened by Sudanese rebels led by a Muslim mystic, Mohammed Ahmad al-Mahdi. Gordon arrived in Khartoum on February 18th 1884, as governor-general of the Sudan.

He made a number of suggestions and proposals to both London and Cairo. He proclaimed the independence of the Sudan; he permitted retention of slaves (bowing to the inevitable); he demanded that Turkish troops should be despatched to his assistance; he asked permission to confer personally with the Mahdi and he desired to be allowed, if he thought it necessary, to take action south of Khartoum. None of his requests were granted.

By March, he had managed to evacuate some 2,500 people from Khartoum, down the Nile. On April 12th, the attack on Khartoum began. On the 16th, he sent his last telegram before the wires were cut. He complained bitterly of the inaction of the British government.

Gordon had few resources but managed to do quite a lot with what he had. He converted his river steamers into ironclads, built new ones, laid land mines, placed wire entanglements, sent out frequent sorties and kept up the spirits of his men by awarding medals for bravery. But all the while his followers were dying of disease and famine. And the net of the Mahdi was tightening.

And still London argued and procrastinated. In April, the need for a relief expedition was pressed upon the British government but with no success. In May, public opinion demanded help for their hero. Many members of the two houses of parliament concurred. But there were still not enough support. The vote in the house was lost.

But at last, it was finally decided to send a relief expedition from Cairo on August 5th. On September 1st, the commander of the expedition, Lord Wolseley, was ready to leave England. From then on, everything that could be done was done. But the delay was fatal.

On September 9th, Gordon sent the last Europeans in Khartoum down the Nile. The small party included the British Consul and *The Times* correspondent. Their steamer was treacherously wrecked by sympathisers of the Mahdi and the passengers murdered. That same day, in far-away England, the first ship of the relief expedition sailed from port. But there had been no attempt to send a flying force to raise the siege.

Meanwhile Gordon was doing his best to keep his depleted (and sometimes mutinous) force on the alert. But all were now famished and living on rats and old shoe leather. The number dead amounted to 1,900 and there were many wounded. They could hold out no longer. When the siege was finally raised, the Mahdi's men raced through the streets, putting everyone - including Gordon - to the sword.

But how did Gordon die? There were many stories, contradicting each other. Some said he had been shot. Others that he fought to the last with sword and revolver. According to John Pollock's *Gordon, the Man Behind the Legend,* the manner of Gordon's death was revealed 43 years after the event. A young Englishman in the Sudan Political Service got to talking to a group of villagers. An elderly man, at the back of the circle that had gathered, butted in on the conversation. 'I saw Gordon die', he said.

They found him waiting on the top of the palace steps. 'He looked at us and we looked at him', the old man said. 'Then he tore open his tunic and said, "Strike! Strike hard" and somebody threw a spear and it was all over'.

Lt-Col Graham Seton Hutchinson, author of the *Gordon and the Gordon Boys* says quite simply: 'The circumstances that produced him were exceptional. There will never be another Gordon.'

Gordon was indeed a one-off. Modest and retiring, he would nevertheless speak out forcefully when he believed himself to be right. He had a lifelong disdain for wealth and praise, not caring what anyone said of him - good or bad. He had a most attractive personality and won over everyone he met. He was quick tempered though also forgiving almost to a fault. Although his beliefs were somewhat mystical, he was a true Christian and believed in doing whatever he thought to be God's will.

There are still many reminders of Charlie Gordon in the Medway towns of Kent. His official residence, Fort House, was demolished in the Second World War but the gardens Gordon opened to the public are still there. There are Gordon Roads in Brompton, Chatham, Gillingham, Hoo and Strood and a Gordon Terrace in Rochester. There is also a Gordon Hotel in the High Street, Rochester.

In Brompton Barracks there is a statue of Gordon on a camel, which is identical to a statue, which once stood at Khartoum and is now outside the Gordon School in Woking.

The largest collection of Gordon Memorabilia in the world, from his days in China, Egypt and the Sudan, can be seen in the Royal Engineers Museum in Gillingham.

Whatever would the 'Kernal' have made of it all?

Rochester hero drew crowd of over 10,000

PERCY HENRY GORDON (C1886-1912)

On November 3rd 1912, an estimated 10,000 people thronged the streets of Rochester to commemorate an act of bravery that was both heroic and tragic. 'The Esplanade from the High Street far into the Baker's Walk and the Churchfield Road was one seething mass of humanity', according to the *Chatham, Rochester and Gillingham Observer.* The local nobility came in the form of the Countess of Darnley, who 'gracefully performed the ceremony'. The Mayor was there and also representatives from the local fire brigades, the police, postmen, the Medway Swimming Club and others.

The crowds and the celebrities had come to unveil a commemorative plaque to a young hero called Percy Henry Gordon, whose one heroic act had caught the public's imagination.

The story was quite simple. It took place on Good Friday, April 5th 1912. Gordon, aged 26, from Bermondsey, and Charles May, of Clapham, had come down to Rochester for a daytime excursion. They had seen the sights of the city and were sitting on the Esplanade pier, waiting for a train back to London. The time was about 5.15 pm. May was for moving off but Gordon wanted to pause for a bit. 'This is one of the finest views I have ever seen in my life', he said.

There were a lot of children milling about, running up and down the steps of the pier. May remarked at how dangerous this seemed to be. Suddenly there was a shout and one of the children rushed up the steps and said that a small girl had fallen into the water. Gordon didn't hesitate. Ripping off his overcoat, jacket and waistcoat, he dived straight in after her. He swam to the child and held her in his arms. They were carried down the river for some distance. After about five minutes, she was picked up by Herbert Hughes, of 4 Brunswick Road, Maidstone. He had rowed from a motor launch in a dinghy.

The story should have ended there except that Gordon, as soon as he had handed over the child, sank and drowned, about nine or ten yards from the lower end of the pier and only some three boat-lengths from the dinghy. His body was recovered 'by means of grapnels' half-an-hour later. At the inquest, it was learned that Gordon's health was good and that he had learned to swim the previous year. But by the look of his face, it seemed likely that he had been seized by cramp. The tide was running strongly at the time and the water was choppy.

The Observer revealed that Gordon was an assistant warehouseman at Nicholson's wharves, Lower Thames Street, London. The little girl, Dorothy Foster, was taken to her parents' house, at 91 Mill Terrace, Frindsbury, little the worse for her adventure.

At the inquest, the coroner summed up by saying that Gordon had died the death of a hero. There was no more noble way of departing this life than in endeavouring to save the life of another, he said. The conduct in this case was somewhat in accord with the great act of self-sacrifice, which was celebrated on Good Friday and his act was all the more worthy in as much as he gave his life for that of a child. It was also said that Gordon was expecting to be married soon and that his fiancée was at the inquest.

The fine memorial tablet, unveiled before the crowd of thousands, can still be seen on the castle wall, at the scene of the tragedy. The Royal Humane Society granted an In Memoriam Certificate and the Carnegie Trust awarded the hero a Bronze Medal. It was said, 'why do we consider this young man a hero? Because he thought not of himself, not of the coldness of the water, not of the strong tide then ebbing or the different currents that had to be contended against in this part of the river. He thought only of his fellow-creature who was in danger of losing her life. He revealed to us a great act of love and service'.

Some of the 10,000 people who came to pay their respects.

In the Dragon's Pulpit

HENRY WHITFIELD GUINNESS (1908-1996)

A man of immense personal courage, Henry Guinness - who spent his last days in Kent - was to be sorely tested during some of the most turbulent years of China's recent history. He was a member of the famous Guinness family who, over the years has produced so many successful brewers, bankers and missionaries. Henry, who belonged to the last category, was born on April 18th 1908, in Kaifeng, Henan province, China.

Both his parents were missionaries in China, his father being the first missionary in the area. His mother, Jane af Sandeburg,

Henry Guiness as a young man in 1931

came from a noble Swedish family and had met his father after the collapse of the Boxer Rebellion at the turn of the nineteenth century

Kaifeng was a filthy city and at the age of two the young Henry contracted tuberculosis and had frequent bouts of dysentery. His parents took the painful decision to send him home to Sweden for his safety. His pet toy was a stuffed elephant, which he clutched for comfort. However, on the trans-Siberian railway, he tossed his toy out of the window. Talking about the trip shortly before he died, he said that he expected the elephant ... 'To trundle along as elephants do and keep up with the train'.

Henry first went to England when he was 11. He was sent to St Lawrence College, in Ramsgate, Kent. He was already trilingual, fluent in English, Swedish and Mandarin.

His father died when he was 17. It was a time when he took stock of his life and what he wanted to do. His resolve to return to China as a missionary surprised everyone including his housemaster, for at school he was considered among the least reverend pupils. He had a reputation for tomfoolery and couldn't resist a dare.

He decided to skip university and first took a job in business in London for a year. He followed this by going to the Bible Training Institute (now the International Christian College in Glasgow) then joined the China Inland Mission (its name changed to OMF International with its UK headquarters in North London, now in Borough Green). In the autumn of 1931, he sailed from Tilbury with 70 other new recruits.

In China, he began his mission in rural Honan, walking or cycling between villages. He had a silver cornet, a family heirloom that he had taught himself to play in Glasgow. After a crowd had gathered to hear him play, he would put down the cornet and begin to spread the word of God.

Henry was also an amateur inventor. He took boys camping and showed them how to make pinhole cameras and model aeroplanes, while addressing such questions as 'why should we believe in the Bible?' At night, he read to them from the Gospel of St John.

Henry saw great opportunities for evangelism and prayed for a co-worker. That night, a burglar broke into his house. The missionary, dressed only in his pyjamas, confronted the man, sat him down with the Bible and had him read the St John's Gospel. After little more than an hour, the thief professed that he wanted to become a Christian. They prayed together.

The next morning, Henry left his burglar in the house while he went on his usual rounds. Returning at lunchtime, he invited the man to become his co-worker - and the offer was accepted.

Early in the 1930s, a cholera epidemic was responsible for some 150,000 deaths. Added to this, there were crop failures and an earthquake. In 1933, the Japanese invaded Shanghai and Communist armies began taking Christians captive. Others, such as Alfred Bosshardt, featured elsewhere in this book, were forced to join Mao's famous long march.

Despite the many dangers, Henry kept himself fit by a lifetime habit of cold showers and long runs of up to 40 miles at a time. In at least one incident, he certainly needed his fitness. After preaching at an inn, he overheard a group of brigands plotting to put him down a well. Aware of such constant dangers, he had previously made a close inspection of a means of escape. He had spotted a small niche in the outside wall, which would give him a foothold out. Strolling nonchalantly across the yard, he suddenly sprang to the foothold, got over the ten-feet high wall and jumped down the other side. The town gates were thrown open and dogs and brigands followed in his wake. But Henry was too fast for them all, outdistanced them and reached the next town, about four miles away.

In 1938, he married Dr Mary Taylor, a graduate of Glasgow University. They settled in Kaifeng where Mary worked in the hospital that Henry's father had founded.

After Pearl Harbour, they moved to Xiangcheng, a small town in South Henan. It was hardly a good time to be in China and the following years were to test the Guinnesses' enormous courage and endurance to the limit. For three years there was drought, famine and hyperinflation. Their funds were so small they could hardly afford to buy rice. Many Chinese families 'discarded' their youngest child, being unable to feed him or her. The Guinnesses loved children and took in as many of these strays as they could manage, sharing out their own limited rations.

Rains came at last, only to cause the most serious flooding. Then there were the locusts, millions of them. And as if this wasn't enough, the Guinnesses could see the war coming closer and closer.

The couple wore Chinese dress and following local custom, they christened their sons with the same ending to their names - Gerald, Oswald and Reginald. Sadly, only Oswald survived. Gerald died of dysentery when he was three years old and Reginald died soon afterwards, at seven months. But there was little time for mourning. They had to flee the following day, to escape the invading Japanese.

The Guinnesses were transferred to Dublin, where of course the family was well known. They briefly represented the mission there but a telegram from Honan urged their return to China. The Sino-Japanese war had come to an end.

From 1947, the Guinnesses were based in Nanjing, where they played a key role at the great student centre. The Chinese Inter-Varsity Fellowship was then the largest movement of its kind in the world. Madam Chiang Kai-shek was among the speakers and there was still a great thirst for religion and knowledge of the outside world. The Communists, however, were gaining ever greater power and in 1949, they closed the centre.

Henry gave Bible classes to the students at his home, which at first were a great success. But then the Communist indoctrination meetings began and the new power in the land had no time for religion. Public trials were held and mass executions followed with as many as 300 townspeople shot every day.

Chou En-lai had a message for the Guinnesses and everyone like them: 'While China is putting its house in order, it is undesirable for guests to be present'. Henry and Mary realised that their presence was becoming a threat to their Chinese friends. So they made plans to pack for home and were amongst the last to leave in 1952. During the last few months they were virtually under house arrest. As an example of their state of privation, a cup of tea was for Sundays only - the rest of the week they quenched their thirst with water.

For the next ten years, Henry represented the mission in Glasgow, until he was able to return to Asia - to Malaysia and then Taiwan. He retired in 1975, living first in St Albans, later in Pembury in Kent. He always kept up his zeal for evangelism and made many friends, especially among the Chinese restaurant community. Mary died in 1993.

Henry never lost his love for China. In April 1995 - despite severe arthritis and having had three hip operations - he went back for a visit, to Xiangcheng and Kaifeng. He was delighted to meet many old friends but disappointed he was unable to find his sons' graves.

It is believed that Henry's secret wish was to be able to die in China, where he was born. Instead, he finally passed away in OMF's Cornford House, Cornford Lane, in Pembury, Kent, on February 17th 1996, aged 87. His surviving son, Os, is a writer and a devout follower of the Christian faith. He is based in the United States.

A final word comes from David Ellis, former National Director of the OMF: 'Henry Guinness was brave and determined. It was typical of him that on his last Sunday on earth he should force his feet into his shoes to go to church, when his heels were raw and turning gangrenous'.

In everything he did, Henry Guinness never lacked the necessary courage of a true hero.

* * *

A Whisper from Death - Special Agent in the French Resistance

RICHARD HESLOP (1908-1973)

Courage comes in many forms. 'It takes a special kind of courage to enter an occupied country in wartime and build organised resistance against the conquerors. It is the sort of courage that transcends fear, that turns cowardice into bravery, and that can accept the unnerving and narrow borderline between life and death. Colonel Richard Heslop had courage of this kind.'

This was written by Heslop's publicist on the flyleaf of his autobiography, *Xavier*,

Richard Heslop, code-named Xavier, in 1944

his code name as special agent. He brought something else vital to the job. In Professor M R D Foot's account of the activities of the special agents in France, he wrote that Heslop had 'that mesmeric quality that makes men follow another man through flood, through fire...Xavier will be a name of power for centuries in the Alpine hamlets that know him.'

Heslop/Xavia - who spent his last years in Harbledown and Herne Bay in Kent - was sent to France in the Second World War to train and organise resistance groups against the enemy. It was a life in which you lived on your nerves, aware that any minute, an unknown Nazi sympathiser could turn you in to the Gestapo. Capture, torture and a slow death were the inevitable consequences of a wrong move, a slip of the tongue. The job in hand was sabotage, espionage, theft and even murder.

Heslop began as a raw recruit in Britain's SOE - the Special Operations Executive - later called the Intelligence Corps. He was put through a rigorous training course and given a new persona, which included his cover as a travelling jeweller. For this, he was even taught how to handle precious stones, how to value them, and everything necessary for him to appear a real professional. He carried about £250 worth of uncut diamonds. This cover had another advantage. It also enabled him to carry around large sums of money, forbidden to a normal person.

He memorised an entire false life so that under interrogation, his story would be secure. At first, under test interrogation, he could easily be tricked into giving real information, rather than his cover. But gradually he got better. He realized that his life - and the lives of others - could depend on it. And he made it stick - so it came to him as second nature.

Heslop and the other recruits learned how to send messages in code and how to survive in open countryside. For this, their instructor was the royal gamekeeper on the Sandringham Estate. They learned from him how to poach birds and fish, and how to build a shelter of branches and leaves. (He also told them that if they took to poaching the royal game parks after the war, he would have no sympathy!).

Heslop learned how to sit in a restaurant with his back to the wall, so nobody could shoot at him from behind. Wherever he was, he had to be aware of an escape route, should it be necessary. He learned how to handle all types of weapons and sabotage gear - how to keep plastic explosives in his pocket without risk of it going off.

The suit he wore was in the French style, with the labels of a well-known French tailor sewn in. And of course all the clothes had to be well worn in.

Because he had weak ankles, Heslop was not parachuted into France. Instead, he was flown to Gibralter, then taken by submarine to the French coast and set ashore by dinghy. His chief had a final cheerful farewell: if he was captured, there was nothing Britain could do, they had never heard of him. 'That's the way it is,' he was told. 'Good luck!'

Heslop got safely to France but was picked up in consequence of breaking one of the SOE's strictest rules. It had been drummed into them that an agent never hung around when an appointment wasn't kept. Heslop did just this and was surrounded by a group of plain-clothes police.

He and his colleagues were incarcerated for several months by the French Vichy regime. When the time was approaching for the German Gestapo to take over, both men were suddenly released. The Resistance found a number of French police who were prepared to look the other way in difficult circumstances. Heslop was quickly back in England.

He was soon ready for his second mission to France. He wrote that 'meetings with Gestapo agents had turned me into a professional, able to hate, but hate with a coldness that kept my temper under control.'

Wiser and more careful, he spent the rest of the war in France. He was involved in training and organising agents, in guerrilla warfare, de-railing trains, snatching food supplies, sabotaging factories, and shooting Germans whenever the got the opportunity. He also organised drops of weapons, medicine, and food - carried out by the RAF.

Throughout Heslop's book, *Xavier,* the reader is often aware of the kind of tension the Resistance was living under. But much else is recalled without too much emotion. The actions and the risks come over as simply a way of life - albeit a highly dangerous one.

For his work in the Resistance, Heslop was awarded the Distinguished Service Order, the Legion d'Honour, the Croix de Guerre with three palms (equivalent to being mentioned three times in dispatches) and the American Medal of Freedom with palm (the palm indicating a way in which an American medal was given to a foreigner).

After the war, Colonel Heslop went to East Africa as a district officer in the Colonial Service, then to Malaya. He returned to live in Harbledown near Canterbury, and moved to Herne Bay in 1963. His last home was at 15 Mickleburgh Hill, Herne Bay. He died on Wednesday January 17th 1973, at Nunnery Fields Hospital, Canterbury. He was 65.

Meet the Real James Bond, from Bromley

Duane Tyrrel Hudson (1910-1995)

When Ian Fleming was casting around for models for his super hero, James Bond, he not unnaturally thought of the secret agents he had met during his time in Intelligence during the Second World War. He wanted a cool 'gentleman', who knew his wines as well as he knew his women. Agent OO7 also had to be tough, able to live on his wits, and be somebody who could look after himself as well with his fists as with a gun. Who should be the role model?

There was one man who fitted these requirements as snugly as a kid glove over a clenched fist. That was Kent-born Duane Tyrrel Hudson - Bill to his friends. Hudson was tall and good looking and an outstanding athlete who had played rugby for London University and had boxed as a heavyweight in student and ABC championships. He was tough and intelligent and also known as something of a ladies' man.

Hudson was born into a South African family in Bromley, Kent on August 10th 1910. He was educated at St Andrews College, Grahamstown and then at the Royal School of Mines in London. In 1935, he worked in Yugoslavia as manager of an antimony mine, where he learned his fluent Serbo-Croat. He travelled the country prospecting and formed warm relationships with the local Serb population. Much to his delight, many of the peasants he met were First World War veterans, who showed considerable regard for their British allies.

In 1936, Hudson married Ada Proskurnikov, a Russian prima ballerina, one of a number of White Russians who had fled the Soviet Union after the revolution. But she found it difficult to adapt to a life in Yugoslavia and they divorced. Hudson never married again.

After the outbreak of war, Hudson was asked to join Section D - the British secret service branch set up to wage 'ungentlemanly warfare' and which was later incorporated into the Special Operations Executive (SOE).

At the beginning of the war, Yugoslavia was still at peace but Hitler had long had his eyes on the country and it was reckoned to be only a matter of time before the long-awaited invasion took place. Yugoslavs were already taking sides. A British agent had been shot and Hudson himself was lucky to escape with his life when a pro-German Croat planted a bomb beneath Hudson's office.

Germany invaded Yugoslavia on April 6th 1941. Five months later, on

September 20th 1941, Hudson was taken by submarine to Montenegro and then lowered with a canoe just off the coast. Years later, in October 1984, in an interview he gave to the (South African) Sunday Times, Hudson attacked the way that the SOE had handled things. 'They just pitchforked me into that country without any preparation whatsoever', he told the reporter. His briefing was unsatisfactory and his radio equipment, he complained, was hopelessly inadequate. It was ludicrously heavy and could only operate from AC power.

Col. Duane Tyrrel Hudson

His orders were to: 'Discover who is fighting the enemy and to co-ordinate all elements of resistance'. It took Hudson just five weeks to report the basic facts and to meet most of the people who would be involved in SOE operations.

The first Yugoslavs he met were some shepherds who promised to take him to the leader of the Partisans. After a two-week trek through enemy territory, he was taken to meet the then unknown Jodip Broz Tito. Tito had set up a Soviet-style People's Republic as a first stage revolution against the Royalists.

Hudson was impressed: 'I found Tito to be cool and rational with a lot of support from the people'. Asked by Tito what he planned to do in the country, Hudson answered that he had come 'to co-ordinate the resistance against the enemy.'

Hudson was immediately aware of the enmity between the two groups of resistance fighters. Tito told Hudson that the Royalist leader of the Chetniks, Draza Mihailovic, was collaborating with the Axis powers. Despite this, Hudson was determined to assess both groups. Besides, Mihailovic had been appointed by the Yugoslav government-in-exile in London to exercise sole authority in its name.

Although both groups were supposed to be fighting the Germans, they were also at odds with one another. Hudson was the only agent to meet the leaders of both groups.

After talking to the Partisans, he moved on to visit the Royalist winter headquarters. 'Mihailovic blew his top and spoke of Tito in violent terms', Hudson recalled. 'He told me there was no support for Tito'.

Who was he to believe? Mihailovic saw his task as one of a shield, protecting his people from reprisals. Tito was the opposite, a sword who attacked the Axis without giving a damn about reprisals.

Shortly before his arrival at the Chetnik HQ, the British had dropped arms and supplies to the Royalists. But instead of using them against Germans, they turned on Tito's Partisans.

Hudson's prediction that the differences between the two groups would break out into armed warfare came true, with the Partisans gaining the upper hand. The Royalists asked for a truce but while this was being negotiated, the Germans drove the Partisans deep into Montenegro and Mihailovic and his men were forced underground.

In the circumstances, Hudson advised London to call a halt to the drops of materials to the Chetniks. Angered by this and the fact that Britain no longer seemed to be taking an interest in its agent, Mihailovic 'cut him out' and ordered Hudson away from his lines. Hudson was thus left to fall back on his own wits in an area now thick with Germans, who were making savage reprisals against the local population. Villages were burnt and 100 Serbs hanged for every one German killed. Hudson later recalled: 'I did not witness actual executions but regularly saw piles of bodies of peasants shot dead and hanged'.

He was ambushed and had his horse shot from under him. He was captured twice, once by Quislings and once by bandits. He escaped both times but lost his radio and most of his belongings. He survived with the help of ordinary Yugoslavs who gave him shelter and shared their meagre rations, ignoring the threat of German reprisals. Nevertheless, by April 1941 he was suffering acute mental anguish and nearly starving.

Mihailovic had regained contact with London and assured the SOE that the Chetniks had assumed power in the civil war. So once more, the Royalists began receiving drops of money, supplies and Yugoslav personnel. In May, Hudson was invited to rejoin the Chetniks.

The following month, Mihailovic moved his force to Italian occupied Montenegro, where he became effectively a guest of the local Chetniks, who were co-operating with the Italians against the Partisans. However, the savage German reprisals had had their effect and Mihailovic refused to continue active warfare against the Axis. In this alone, he left himself wide open to later accusations of collaboration with the enemy.

German reprisals had done little to stop the fighting carried out by the Partisans and Hudson came to realise that they were the stronger force. However, when he passed on this opinion to the British, he was simply not believed. He was accused of becoming unhinged by his ordeal, he was politically naïve, or simply a leftist.

In late 1942, Colonel Bailey was sent out to check on Hudson's intelligence and he found himself agreeing on every point. Bailey got no further with Mihailovic than Hudson had. Hudson stayed on as political advisor first to Bailey and then to Brigadier Armstrong. By now the Deakin and Maclean missions to the Partisans had confirmed what Hudson had been saying for two years. In December 1943, it was Churchill who took the decision to drop Mihailovic and support Tito.

Hudson saw the terrible waste caused by the enmity between the two Yugoslav parties and made a plea for unity - for a final campaign against the Germans. He knew that the Partisans were predominant in Bosnia and Montenegro. But there were few in Serbia where most people were anti-communist and there were some 100,000 Chetniks under arms. Hudson proposed that the two forces be merged; Mihailovic would have to go but Tito would also have to make concessions. In May 1944, Hudson flew home to put his view to Churchill and Eden. But Tito - now having the support of both Britain and the Soviet Union - was in no mood to make concessions. In the ensuing bloodbath, the Chetniks were totally destroyed.

Hudson's last SOE mission found him parachuted into Poland with several other officers and an interpreter. Owing to pilot error, the men fell heavily and were all concussed. Upon regaining consciousness, they were captured by the Russians. They were soon freed, however, were royally entertained in Moscow and provided with a box at the Bolshoi.

For his heroic work in the Second World War Hudson was awarded the DSO, appointed OBE and mentioned in dispatches. He ended the war as a full colonel.

After the war, Hudson considered going back to his mining operations in Yugoslavia but, because of his association with Mihailovic, would have been arrested as a war criminal. In 1946, when Mihailovic was put on trial as a traitor, Hudson offered to speak in his defence but was turned down. Mihailovic was sentenced to death and executed.

Hudson went to South Africa where he discovered a deposit of tungsten and mined it for a while. He sold out so profitably that he was able to live on the proceeds for the rest of his life. He divided his time between Durban and London, where he had a flat overlooking St James Palace.

He did, however, take up pecan-nut farming on an estate he had inherited at Muden in the KwaZulu-Natal Midlands. He died on November 1st 1995, in Durban and left the bulk of his considerable estate to local charities

For all his success, Hudson suffered from bouts of depression and was haunted by his failure to mediate between the Partisans and the Chetniks.

Lifeboat Heroes

HOW IT ALL BEGAN - EARLY DAYS

For British seamen and for those having anything to do with the sea, it was perhaps the most important meeting that ever took place. On March 4th 1824, at the *City of London Tavern,* a number of dignitaries presided over by the Archbishop of Canterbury and including William Wilberforce, inaugurated the Royal National Lifeboat Institution - then known as the National Institution for the Preservation of Life from Shipwreck.

Men and women of the RNLI have ever since done a remarkable job in putting their lives on the line rescuing seafarers in difficulty. Although some of the great legendary rescues have taken place in the teeth of savage gales, huge seas, and icy temperatures, most of the work carried out by the RNLI actually happens in summer at a time when most people go to the sea. Swimmers are exhausted, wind-surfers capsize, or children in inflatables are blown out to sea.

In all-weather stations, rescues do nevertheless take place in the foulest weather mother nature can produce. And despite the obvious dangers, the number wanting to be lifeboatmen always exceeds the need. Lifeboatmen - and increasingly this also includes women - can be called upon day or night, 365 days a year. The RNLI has first call on their time and their employers know this and respect it. Nobody does it for the money.

Allowances are more or less token. For the crew on a service (that's a rescue) it's £9 for the first hour and £2.50 for each subsequent hour. On an exercise, it's £9 for the first three hours and £2.60 for each hour after that, to a maximum of ten hours. Shore helpers, those that assist with launchings and recoveries of the boats, are on a lower rate.

Since the beginning of the RNLI, women have played an important role, particularly in the launchings - that is moving the lifeboat across the beach and into the sea. Until the comparatively recent arrival of tractors, it was necessary to manually drag the lifeboat across the beach and into the water. It was backbreaking work and often needed to be carried out in the worst of weathers.

In the days before radio, the women helpers - cold, soaked and exhausted - had to huddle around a stove, waiting for the return of the lifeboats and the important task of recovery. And it was hard work. In 1933, in the days of sail and before the arrival of the electric winch, it took 30 people over two hours to haul the boat up.

In 1979, the last two lifeboat launchers, Mrs. Doris Tart and Mrs. John Bates, both from Dungeness, were awarded the Institution's Gold Badge for their outstanding services. Mrs. Tart had been a shore helper for 44 years and Mrs. Bates for 37. Mrs. Tart's mother and her aunt had also been awarded Gold Badges in 1953 in recognition of 50 years' service as shore helpers.

One outstanding rescue gives an idea of what Kent lifeboat crews go through when they respond to the cry for help from those in peril on the sea.

'When the adrenaline gets going, there's no time to think of the risks'.

PETER THOMAS, RNLI BRONZE MEDAL (1949-)

'I've known men crushed to death doing what I did', former lifeboat man Peter Thomas told me, sitting inside the two railway carriages he and his wife have converted into a cosy, comfortable home at Dungeness. He wasn't boasting. It was the kind of risk that lifeboat men frequently face. Peter would never brag about anything like that. As with most lifeboat men, he is a modest man.

But he was also proud of what he did. Proud of the letter he received from his MP, of the newspaper interviews, of the coveted Blue Ribbon he received from the shipping company of the man whose life he had saved. And proud - most of all - of the RNLI bronze medal he received, presented personally by the Duke of Kent.

And how did he win that medal?

It was early afternoon on February 11th 1974 - often the coldest time of the year. The alarm was raised - a ship was in trouble. Nowadays, lifeboat men are issued with pagers. But in 1974, they were summoned by telephone. It was based on the cascade principle. The Honorary Secretary rang the coxswain, the coxswain's wife rang the mechanic, and the mechanic's wife rang the next member of the crew. And so on. Within minutes, 20 or 30 people had been alerted.

Peter explained how his clothes were always ready. Normal people probably hang up their things in the wardrobe before going to bed. With a lifeboat man, all his clothes - jumpers, thermals, leggings, sea boots, top coat - are laid out on the floor ready to be pulled on. Every split second counts.

On this particular February afternoon, the full crew had arrived at the lifeboat, waiting for orders. Peter noticed there were more people crowding round than he'd ever seen. More in fact than anybody could remember. These neighbours, living by the sea, realised just what it meant to take out the lifeboats in this kind of weather. They knew the risks the crew was taking - and feelings of worry, concern and fear were running high.

The coxswain rang the coastguard for a situation report.

The ship in trouble was a Danish coaster - the 400-ton Mercandia vessel, *Merc Texco* - with a deck cargo of timber up in the bow. The water had come over the bow and shifted the timber and a crew member had been badly injured. He had been caught across his thighs and his left ankle was broken. He was in agony and needing medical treatment desperately.

A helicopter, based about two and a half miles away, had attempted to let down a wire, so that the injured man could be winched up. But after failing in several attempts, the cable was released and the helicopter flew back to its base.

The helicopter reported to the Coast Guard, who in turn rang Peter's Honorary Secretary. He reported to the lifeboatmen. But the final decision - whether to go or stay - always rests with the coxswain. In this case, despite the awful weather, he gave the go-ahead. In the past, launching the boat could take hours of back-breaking work. With modern techniques, launching takes about half a minute. The lifeboat hit the water at around 25 mph.

Weather conditions were the worst Peter had ever known. Winds were between 80 and 100 mph and waves as high as 35 feet smashed down upon them. There were available life lines for everybody to be attached to the boat but nobody used them - if the boat capsized, it was too easy to be caught. There was a temporary hold-up as the lifeboat got stuck on a sand bank and had to be freed. They then steamed towards the ship with the injured man.

When they reached the 42-feet long *Merc Texco,* they found about 20 other ships in the immediate vicinity. There appeared to be little co-operation from the skipper of the ship with the injured man so the coxswain asked for a volunteer to board the ship and find out what could be done. Peter immediately agreed to go.

Peter spoke quite calmly, matter-of-factly, about what happened next. The seas were so strong; it was hard to direct the lifeboat in any one direction. You were on the crest of a high wave one minute, then crashing down into the ocean trough the next. Often as helpless as a bobbing cork. Conditions were bitter. The wind seemed to cut into the skin and immediately draw tears. Your clothes were soaked through with icy water. You were in pain, ice-cold pain but so busy you hardly noticed it. Somehow, with all this going on, the lifeboat was manoeuvred alongside the steamer - as near to the side as it was possible to go without being hurled against it.

The pilot's ladder - hanging down the side of the steamer - swung crazily. Peter grabbed at it. With both boats rolling badly, the ladder would be in the air one moment, smashing down onto the ship's side the next. And Peter crashed with it. He was battered and hurt.

The pain of the hurt combined with the pain of the cold. He knew, any fool could see it, there was a strong possibility that the two dangerously rolling ships would crash together. The man in between would be pulverised. So much he knew instinctively. But there was no time to think about it. No time to figure anything out. Like with most lifeboatmen, nothing mattered but the job in hand, the rescue. He could feel the adrenaline coursing through his body. There was no time to feel scared.

The ladder hadn't been designed for sea boots, which Peter was wearing. So he had half a foot on the rungs, half a foot off. When he had nearly reached the top, strong hands reached down and pulled him on board.

The injured man, a Dane, had been carried in a stretcher up to the bridge, ready for the helicopter. He now had to be brought down again so he could be lowered down the side of the boat. The man was in agony, despite two powerful shots of morphine - the highest dose that could safely be given. It was now about 4pm, getting dark. Someone offered the injured man a drink. Peter put up his hand to stop it. No drink, nothing! He knew the medical rules. The man would soon be having an operation with anaesthetic, for which he would need an empty stomach.

Peter supervised lowering the man over the side. As he was telling me this, he grinned. 'Sounds easy, doesn't it?' And he reminded me that winds were now at a steady 85 mph or so - not gusting to that speed but steady. It was hard to keep upright and as he was letting himself down the pilot's ladder he slipped and fell - fortunately into the arms of one of the lifeboat's crew. The casualty was given some pain-relieving gas (which seemed to have little effect). Somehow they got back to base. The man was immediately rushed off to hospital. Peter felt his responsibility at an end. Now was the time to look back and be scared.

There was a question I'd been wanting to ask Peter ever since I knew I was going to meet him. 'Why do you do it?' Why do you leave your warm comfortable home and go into the worst possible weather conditions - for what? It was certainly not for money. Apart from the mechanic who received a salary, the others were paid a nominal pound for "getting the boat wet" then 50p an hour. (Today's rates are much higher but nobody does it for the money). So why did he do it?

'It's in the blood,' Peter said. 'I was a fisherman for 26 years, from the time I left school. It was a family business. And when my father retired from the lifeboat service, I took his place. As a fisherman, as someone connected with the sea, you always assume that if you get caught out, there will always be someone there to rescue you. It's a personal thing. It's in the blood.'

He continued. 'And when you're out on a job, you aren't really aware of the risks. There is no time to be frightened. The adrenaline gets going You're constantly busy. Everyone knows everyone else's job. You just get on with it.'

And that really was the only explanation I was going to get.

Finally, what about the practical arrangements? For everyone in the service, no matter what their main job is, the lifeboats have first call on their time. All employers know this. And they accept it.

Peter Thomas, being presented with the coverted RNLI bronze medal by the Duke of Kent

The RNLI is an independent voluntary organisation. It lives on donations and gets nothing from the government. They're very proud of their independence.

And women, were there ever any women crews these days? Peter said there was already an all-woman crew at Dungeness. Asked what he thought of the idea, 'No comment' was the most he would say.

One way or another, helping others has always been Peter's way. That's just the man he is. Now he's retired altogether from the sea, his main work is as a ranger employed by the Dungeness Nuclear Power Station. His job is to see that nobody strays past the 'Keep Out' signs.

But in his spare time, Peter is still doing good. He's secretary of the RAOB, the Royal Antediluvian Order of Buffaloes. He says it's an organisation somewhat similar to the Masons, and devotes its time to raising money for good causes. Peter wouldn't really feel happy if he wasn't doing something like this.

It's in the blood.

'The Greatest British Female Mountaineer Between the Wars'

NEA EVERILDA MORIN (1905-1986)

One day in the early years of the last century - the exact date is not chronicled - a small, frightened girl bawled her eyes out for rescue from the top of a sandstone pinnacle of the Wellington Rocks on Tunbridge Wells Common, near where she lived. The child, Nea Everilda Barnard, was rescued by an elderly gentleman. It was a salutary lesson - and not just that it's often more difficult coming down than going up. Never again would Nea call for male assistance.

Nea was born on May 21st 1905, at Headley Down, in Hampshire. She grew up among climbers and learned to love mountains above all things - to be amongst them, to scale them, to climb rocks and teach others to do the same, to introduce beginners and - eventually - to foster and develop this love in her own family.

Nea Morin, at the top of Harrison's Rocks, between Groombridge and Eridge.

In *Women Climbing* by Bill Birkett and Bill Peascod, the authors refer to Nea Morin (her married name) as: 'The greatest British female mountaineer between the wars'. And there were many others with the same opinion.

Her father was a parson who had lost his faith while trying to restore his wife's. As agnostics the family were not well regarded by the many

'Disgusteds of Tunbridge Wells'. But this attitude did little to affect the spirits of Nea and her brothers. She later wrote: 'We were outlaws and rebels and gloried in it'.

Her father was a member of the Alpine Club and the family doctor was Claude Wilson, a one-time president of the club. Wilson's friend, Raymond Bicknell, even offered Nea a loan if one day she wanted to visit alpine country. As it turned out, Nea's first trip to Switzerland was when she was six but the outbreak of the First World War prevented further visits; she made do with the rocks in and around Tunbridge Wells.

Nea had to wait until she was 16, in 1922, before she was able to try her hand at 'real mountains'. This was in the Tirol at St Anton am Arlberg, where the snow-covered peaks towered above her at around 10,000 feet. After the nursery slopes at home, this was 'pure heaven'.

In 1923 and 1925, Nea returned with her family. On guideless climbs with her elder brother, she began to develop her skills and sense of judgment. She discovered that climbing was something she could do really well. If there was a mountain in front of her, it seemed the most natural thing in the world simply to climb it. It never occurred to her that she might fall off. Once, when she was 20, she was to climb the Napes Needle in the Lakes' District with two men friends. It proved too difficult for the men so she simply went up alone.

Determined to make her independent way, she worked for her father - who was now in the antiquarian book business - to save for a trip to the Alps. In 1925, she went to the Dauphine where, without a guide, she scaled the Ecrins.

She was accepted by the Ladies Alpine Club as a graduating member and was given full membership after the following season, 1926, when she was in Chamonix with a friend, Jo Marples. They climbed the Mummery and Ravanel, the Requin and the Geant. Nea also met Jean Morin, one of the best-known climbers of his day and a founder member of the very prestigious *Groupe de Haute Montagne*. She was invited to meet his family in Paris, where she was charmed by their passion for music as well as climbing. In return, she asked her foreign friends over for weekends at Harrison's Rocks, Groombridge, a childhood picnic spot.

In the following year, 1927, Nea and Jo were invited by Jean to join his group in Chamonix. A romance blossomed and grew and at the end of the season, Nea and Jean became engaged; they married several months later. Their daughter, Denise, was born in 1931 and Ian four years later.

After a short time in London, the Morins moved to Paris where Nea became a member of the 'Bleau' group. This group often frequented the rocks at Fontainebleau on the outskirts of Paris. It was here that Nea met Alice Damesme. These two plus Jean's sister, Michaline, were together to write a very important chapter in the book of women's climbing history.

Nea and Jean had attended enough funerals of their friends to realise how uncertain the life of a climber may be. For this reason, for the sake of their children, they agreed that wherever possible they would climb on separate ropes.

In 1933, Alice, Michaline, and Nea considered traversing the Meije in the Dauphine Alps. But at a time of two recent climbing deaths, it was uncertain whether their husbands would give them permission - still considered necessary in 1933!

However, the husbands reluctantly agreed and the three friends set off. They were successful and it proved to be the first major *cordée féminine* climb (a women-only rope).

Come the 1934 season and the women were off again on their own. And despite their men folk's certain conviction that they would fail, they had a very successful climb and reached the summit of all the peaks that they attempted.

In the summer of 1939, Nea and the children settled down in Tunbridge Wells while Jean remained at the Ministry of Armaments in Paris. After the fall of France, Jean made his way to England to join de Gaule. Haunted by the miles of refugees he had seen on French roads, Jean insisted that his family move right out of the potential invasion area of south-east England - they spent the war in North Wales.

In 1943, Jean was killed on a mission with the Free French. Nea hid her grief and looked to the Welsh mountains for comfort. She wrote: 'Since 1940, Wales and the Welsh mountains have played such a large part in my life that, although I love the Alps and always long for their high peaks and glaciers, it is, I think to Wales that I would return for comfort and understanding ... these very old hills somehow gave me confidence, a deep feeling of security, of peace and hope even in the face of tragedy'.

In 1941, she made the first ascent on Clogwyn Y Grochan to be led by a woman and the climb was called 'Nea'. In the guidebook, 'Nea' was described as a 'Magnificent route of great character, 230 feet high and graded "Severe"'.

She also led an ascent of the Curving Crack on Clogwyn du'r Arddu (the Black Cliff), considered by Welsh-based climbers as: 'The most ferocious cliff in Britain'.

Micheline and Nea returned to Chamonix in 1947, to attend the International Climbing Meet. Micheline was one of the organisers and

Nea described herself as a hybrid British-French representative. The two friends climbed the Dent du Requin *en cordée feminine*. Nea's children, Denise, now 16, and Ian, 12 joined them for many family climbs. It also saw the beginning of one of the most successful mother/daughter climbing teams in climbing history.

Writing in the *Alpine Journal,* Janet Adam Smith says: 'It was a privilege to climb with Nea. She was thoroughly competent on snow and ice, but on rock she was beautiful, flowing up with the apparent effortlessness that came from knowing exactly how to use her body, how to plan the moves ahead. She inspired total confidence in her second: behind her, one could tackle climbs one had thought well beyond one's reach'.

In 1959 Nea was invited to join an expedition to the Himalayas, to climb Ama Dablam. The invitation came at a bad time - she had just injured her knee on Harrison Rocks. She nevertheless accepted and in mid-March flew to Delhi and then to Kathmandu.

It was a disastrous expedition. Nea had trouble with both a swollen knee and blistered feet. Then, following a sudden change in the weather, they lost two of their climbers. For Nea, the return journey was even more painful than the outward one. She wrote: 'It seemed as though my bones were grinding in their sockets'.

On her return home, Nea had an operation on her hip, which left her with one leg shorter than the other. But she still continued to climb, walking with the aid of a stick.

Despite her infirmity, she returned again and again to the Alps. She still managed some of the more difficult ascents and climbers who didn't know her were amazed to see this old lady with a stick come off the end of an abseil rope. In 1971, she returned to the Himalayas. She was in considerable discomfort and was taking a doctor's prescription to suppress her appetite. This ability to withstand pain was the price she paid to be in the hills. It was a source of wonder to all those who knew of her heroic courage.

At 70 years of age, she re-climbed 'Nea', the peak she had first ascended in 1941.

In 1982, she suffered a devastating stroke which not even her indomitable will could overcome. The last years in the nursing home were sad ones and she was not able to take in the news that her daughter and climbing partner had been made the first woman president of the Alpine Club.She died in London on July 12th 1986.

At the end of her autobiographical *A Woman's Reach,* Nea considered the dangers of mountain climbing and the courage needed to carry it out.

She wrote also of the friends she had lost. Here is what she said: 'It was inevitable ... that I should think of all the years of my climbing, and more especially of the many friends killed in the mountains. Could climbing be worth this fearful toll of the very best, the most loved and needed, nearly 50 of whom I myself had known? But when I thought back on my own life, on all that mountains meant to me, on all they had brought me in joy and comfort, I knew there could be no doubt of the answer: and those others must surely have felt the same, for they had chosen their way of life:

"Ah! but a man's reach should exceed his grasp
Or what's a heaven for?"'

* * *

The Founder of Modern Alpinism

ALBERT FREDERICK MUMMERY (1855-1895)

What makes a man or woman climb precipitous mountains when death is so often only a slip away? Sir Edmund Hillary is attributed with the now famous: 'Because it's there'. But Dover man Albert Mummery, the foremost climber of the second half of the 19th century, wrote with more passion: 'It has led me into regions of such fairy beauty that the fabled wonders of Zanadu seem commonplace beside them'.

In his several books, he wrote of reaching inaccessible peaks, of hair-breadth escapes in Europe and Asia. Yet in ordinary life Mummery was a quiet, unassuming young man, never boasting of his achievements, which were probably unknown even to his neighbours.

Albert Frederick Mummery

Albert Mummery, the younger of two brothers, was born on September 10th 1855 in Maison Dieu House, Dover, which is now the public library. His father had lived in Deal until he bought the Tanbrook Tannery in Dover, where he later became mayor.

The young Albert, slim, mustached and gangling-limbed, was a natural climber. In some ways he was also frail - he was myopic and had a spine defect that meant he could never carry heavy weights. But he had great muscular strength in arms and legs and little weight of body for them to lift. Friends and fellow climbers have described his great sense of judgment and confidence. It is doubtful if he ever slipped. Nothing flurried or hurried him. Even the weather didn't seem to matter. If need be, he could stay on a mountain ledge out in the open all night.

There are few records of how he started. He probably learned his craft on the chalk cliffs of Kent and Sussex. In 1871, when he was 15, he made his first visit to Switzerland with his parents. He heard the talk that 'there were no more new mountains to climb'. This wasn't literally true except that most of the popular European peaks had been conquered.

He was taken across the Theodule Pass and never forgot his first glimpse of really high mountains. He came down into Valtournanche and saw the Matterhorn. Two decades later, he wrote that he remembered it as if it were yesterday. 'It was shining in all the calm majesty of a September moon and, in the stillness of an autumn night, it seemed the very embodiment of mystery and a fitting dwelling place for the spirits with which old legends people its stone-swept slopes'. And unlike other climbers, he never seemed to lose that first sense of awe.

He did no real climbing on that first visit but within three years he had climbed Monte Rosa and had made the first of his seven ascents of the Matterhorn. Before he was 21, he had climbed Mont Blanc and been up the Matterhorn for the second time. In the summer of 1879, he entered into alpine history with his first ascent on the Matterhorn by a new route - the Zmutt *arete* that other seasoned climbers had called 'totally unassailable'.

In 1879, Mummery, still relatively unknown, asked one of the seasoned guides, the famous Alexander Burgener, to take him up the Zmutt ridge - a particularly difficult challenge. Burgener, knowing nothing of Mummery's skills, suggested they first try a number of less difficult climbs. Mummery agreed and within five days the two returned, the guide quite satisfied that the young man was up to it. Within a week of Mummery's 24th birthday, they had achieved what they set out to do.

In the years 1880 and 1881, the pair made a number of firsts - often tackling a popular mountain by a new and more difficult route.

For many years, Mummery had been blackballed from the Alpine Club. Was it really because, in Victorian parlance, he was in trade! After he did eventually join the club, the blackballing was seen as a major embarrassment by the majority of members. His social position was anyway in little doubt by most people and he was far from being a so-called ordinary tanner. As part owner of a substantial business, he and his family had an established and respected position throughout most of Kent.

During the early 1880s Mummery did very little climbing except for the occasional assent of the chalk cliffs, which stretched between Dover and St Margaret's Bay. He married in 1883 and spent some time 'settling down'. However during these non-climbing years, his thoughts were never far from his life's passion. He was busily planning serious future climbs - this time not to the Alps but to the Caucuses, which run along the Russian and Persian border. In 1887, he initiated his wife into the joys of mountaineering, taking her up the south-western ridge of the Teufelsgrat in the Alps. By the summer of 1888, however, everything was ready for their assault on the Caucuses.

Their journey to the Caucuses was one of exploration as much as anything else. The area was comparatively unknown to Europeans although Elbruz, the highest peak, had been climbed back in 1868. Mummery thoroughly enjoyed the travelling and wrote back to the *Alpine Journal:* 'No other holiday has afforded me half the pleasure'. Mummery and his guide made several successful climbs, the most important of which was probably the great peak of Dych Tau.

In 1890 he was 35, happily married and with a flourishing, profitable business. But he still had a lot to give climbing. In the 1890s Mummery and a few picked companions began to revolutionise mountaineering. They climbed most of the famous peaks in the Alps again but they climbed them without guides - something that had rarely been carried out in the past. They achieved this partly by skill and partly by the knowledge they had of the terrain. It was also the birth of rock climbing (as opposed to mountain climbing) in Britain, which produced a few exceptional cragsmen, whose ability was well equal to that of the normal run of mountain guides.

By this time Mummery was one of the great masters of the art. During the winter of 1894 - perhaps the happiest of his life - he wrote *My Climbs in the Alps and Caucuses*, a joyful celebration of his past 20 years. He wrote modestly in the Preface: 'I fear no contributions to science or topography or learning of any sort are to be found sandwiched in between the story of crags and seracs, of driving storm and perfect weather'.

But he was also preparing for a Himalayan expedition. On June 30th, Mummery sailed for Bombay with two climbing companions, Norman Collie and Geoffrey Hastings. They were heading for Nanga Parbat, a great peak rising to 26,620 feet, in Kashmir, at the Western end of the Himalayas.

After the first few days, Mummery wrote comforting words home to his wife: 'I don't think there will be any serious mountaineering difficulties on Nanga and the peak is much freer from hanging glaciers than I had expected. I fancy that the ascent will be mainly a question of endurance'.

However, after the party had investigated the mountain further, the words home were less confident. It was no longer 'when' we climb Nanga but 'if', and finally, 'even if we don't'.

They decided that to get into better shape, they should try a lower mountain first - of around 19,000 feet. They set off on the morning of August 11th - Mummery, Collie, Hastings, and two Gurkhas called Ragobir and Lor Khan. On the way up there was a potentially dangerous incident. Mummery wrote later: 'the position was a sensational one. We were crossing the steepest ice slope of any great size I had ever been on; below us it shot straight down some 2,000 feet without a break'.

Then Lor Khan - who had no experience of high mountain climbing and wearing only animal skins on his feet - suddenly slipped out of a foot-hold. He hung, suspended, face down on the glistening ice.

Collie wrote later: 'Under him the thin coating of snow peeled off the face of the slope in great and ever-widening masses, gathering in volume as it plunged headlong down the mountain side, finally to disappear over the cliffs thousands of feet below. For the time being I was fascinated by the descending avalanche, my whole mind being occupied with but this one thought, that if Lor Khan began to struggle and jerk at the rope I should without doubt be pulled out of my steps'. But his fears proved groundless. The Ghurka 'never lost either his head or his axe, and was just able to reach with his hand one of the steps out of which he had fallen'.

The danger was over but it had been a close call. Mummery's own endurance was remarkable. He had led the climb from 6,000 to 7,000 feet, cutting steps as he went and was still almost as fresh as when he started. The group returned by another route.

The next day, Mummery was ready to tackle Nanga Parbat. The towering mountain rose above their campsite for thousands of feet, ending in a great snowfield below the summit of the peak itself. Mummery spied a rock-rib that stood out and appeared to be free of the danger of avalanches. Not everyone, however, was yet ready. Hastings was away getting fresh supplies, Lor Khan was doing the same thing and Collie had been weakened by the unaccustomed food.

So only Mummery and Ragobir were ready to set off. Looking at it from today's standards, it was a hazardous and desperate undertaking. There were few reserves and the huge mountain they were about to climb was completely unknown to them. The great rib, thousands of feet in length, was longer and more difficult than anything they had attempted before.

The going was tough. In places, there was snow and ice but mostly it was steep rock, flanked on either side by deep gullies, down which avalanches raced most of the time. For the first two nights, they camped on the rib. On the third day, they saw an avalanche roaring below them -

sweeping away their tent and rucksacks that they had left there.

Then Ragobir fell ill. There was little communication between them - neither spoke a word of the other's language and it turned out that either the Gurkha had brought no food with him or at least had finished it at the first bivouac. He had thus climbed for at least one day with no food inside him; the man was now near to collapse. There was nothing for it but to turn back. They returned down the narrow rib in a single day.

Back in camp, Collie was there and Hastings joined them later. They carefully planned their next move. Time was now against them. The weather was breaking. Mummery and Ragobir had climbed brilliantly. According to Walter Unsworth's *Tiger in the Snow* it had included some of the most difficult rock-climbing ever attempted on a Himalayan mountain. But it was just *too* difficult. They had to find an easier route to the summit. There was still one face of the mountain not explored and this was the northwest, known as the Rakhiot face.

They agreed to split up. Hastings and Collie would shift camp while Mummery and the two Gurkhas would take the more difficult way, up which it would be impracticable to take the supplies. The route proposed by Mummery was steep, unknown and subject to avalanches. Collie advised against it. His long experience told him it might be too dangerous. But Mummery dismissed the warning. 'Don't worry', he laughed. 'I'm not going to risk everything for the sake of an ordinary pass'.

That night Mummery wrote to his wife: 'Well, I shall soon be on my way home ...tomorrow I cross a high pass with the Gurkhas to the Rakhiot nullah. Hastings and Collie go round with the stores'.

On the morning of August 24th Mummery and the two Gurkhas set off, accompanied by two men to carry their rucksacks for part of the way. Later in the day the men returned and Hastings and Collie and the rest set off on the longer route round the ridge. From here, they could see the route that Mummery planned to take and Collie carefully studied the mountain with a powerful telescope. He later wrote that he could see neither steps cut in the mountain nor any sign of Mummery. 'I am therefore of the opinion that Mummery has turned back'. This was what Mummery had told them he would do if the climb proved too difficult. So they sent two of the men round to meet him. Two days later the men returned, having found nothing.

It was now obvious that something had gone badly wrong and they all returned to the Diamirai Glacier, where they still expected to meet Mummery. But there was no trace, even though they continued to search.

Neither Mummery nor the Gurkhas were ever seen again. The most likely cause of their deaths must have been a great avalanche that even Mummery's considerable experience misjudged. Or perhaps, they had slipped and fallen into a crevasse. Mummery was only 40, at the height of his powers. His death was an enormous blow to British mountaineering and a great loss to his many friends in Dover.

It is easy to speculate that Mummery was always prepared for his own death. In *Six Great Mountaineers,* by Ronald W Clark, the author concludes: 'He knew that once a man went beyond a certain point he lived on borrowed time, and he thought that the view from beyond that point made the risk worth while. One feels that he was always ready to pay up should there come, as he might well have put it himself in his rather florid Victorian prose, that demand from the Great Avenger, Death itself.

It came. He paid.'

The Everest Photographer

JOHN BAPTIST LUCIEN NOEL (1890-1989)

Captain John Noel in Tibetan dress, 1913

John Noel, official photographer to the first two full-scale attempts to climb Mount Everest, achieved many things in his crowded life but must have been saddened by missing out on one of his greatest ambitions: to capture the actual conquest of Everest on film.

Noel - who retired to Romney Marsh in Kent - was a young soldier in India before the First World War. He was with the East Yorkshire Regiment stationed in Calcutta and spent his summer leaves wandering the border country of Sikkim, trying to find a way into forbidden Tibet. The aim was to reach Everest. In 1913, he went in disguise. Not as a native, as his Caucasian features would have been a give-away, but as 'a Mohammedan from India'. Taking with him a small party of frontier hillsmen, he finally succeeded in crossing Chorten Nyima La, an unguarded pass to the north of Kangchenjunga, to make his way towards the Arun Valley and, as he hoped, the eastern flanks of Everest.

From Lanbu La, he was able to see a chain of mountains. He named the two most prominent peaks Tarigban (meaning Long Knife) and Guma Raichu (Guma's Tooth). Then as the clouds shifted, directly over the peak of Tarigban, he saw 'a glittering spire top of rock fluted with snow, which according to its magnetic bearing, could be none other than Everest itself'. About 300 to 450 metres of the summit could be seen and Noel reckoned they were separated from Everest by about 95 kilometres of high mountains. His party attempted to approach via the Tashirak Valley but were prevented from going on by hostile Tibetan tribesmen. While attempting to persuade them to let him into the country, he was struck across the face with a whip and actually fired at by a matchlock gun.

In his book, *Through Tibet to Everest,* Noel records his frustration:

'within 40 miles and nearer at that time than any white man had been! I leave you to imagine my chagrin and disappointment.'

By the time he managed to get back to his regiment, he was two months late, making him liable to a court marshal. Noel's unlikely excuse was that his calendar had been washed away during a river crossing. His colonel seemed to swallow this and simply insisted that next time, Noel should bring two calendars.

He came through severe fighting in the First World War and 70 years later, claimed to be one of the last survivors of the British Expeditionary Force (These were the original soldiers who went to France in 1914, and called themselves 'the old contemptibles'). Noel was taken prisoner by the Germans but escaped. He made his way through enemy lines by marching at night and taking his bearings from the star Arcturus.

After the war, he was stationed in Persia to guard the oil fields against a possible threat from the Bolsheviks. When he was sent to do a horseback reconnaissance south of the Caspian Sea, he took his camera equipment with him and made a documentary about the caviar industry.

John Noel's interest in mountains and photography date back to his boyhood. He was the third son of Lieutenant-Colonel the Hon Edward Noel, and grandson of the second Earl of Gainsborough. He was sent to school in Lausanne where, bored with lessons, he began skipping classes to go skating and climbing. He knew the work of the mountain photographer Vittorio Sella and was also much influenced by Herbert Ponting's film of Scott's last Antarctic expedition. He went to see the film 16 times and always reckoned it to be the best documentary ever made.

Noel's mother was a distinguished painter of alpine flowers and she may have wanted her son to follow in her footsteps. She enrolled him in a painting academy in Florence. His father, however, had other ideas and - seeing no future for his son in being an artist - he encouraged the boy to follow his profession in the army. Thus John Noel went to the Royal Military College at Sandhurst and in 1908, was commissioned into the East Yorkshire Regiment.

After the First World War, mountaineers were keen to resume climbing. Noel missed the 1921 reconnaissance to Everest, still being on the shores of the Caspian. But keen to join the 1922 expedition, he resigned his commission, and joined the Alpine Club in the same year. He was invited to give a talk on his 1913 Tibetan journey and this injected sufficient enthusiasm for there to be a new Everest campaign.

His appointment as official photographer to the 1922 expedition was by no means universally welcomed. The 'gentlemen sportsmen' said they did not want the climb to be vulgarised for the cinema. George Mallory said 'he was interested in climbing the mountain, not in being an actor in a film'.

But Noel soon won them over by his efficiency, enthusiasm, and co-operative ways. He was also a devout Catholic and came to be known as 'St Noel of the Cameras.' The leader of the expedition, General Bruce, said: 'There is no more thorough member of the expedition'. Noel wrote later: 'Mallory quite liked my picture-making toys'. Noel always greeted the members of the team with flasks of hot tea, after their climb.

At Base Camp, Noel set up a specially designed tent where he processed some 5,500 metres of film in lined plywood tanks, drying it over a yak dung fire. He managed to haul his cameras up to the North Col, some 23,000 feet above sea level - at that time, a record.

In the 1924 expedition, John Noel was all set to make his fortune and he staked everything, confident of success. He paid £8,000 - an immense sum for the first quarter of the last century - for all photographic rights to the expedition, or £6,000 for film rights, payable in advance. The Everest Committee accepted the sum with alacrity. Noel formed a company, Explorers Films Ltd, to raise the money. He hired his own porters and set up a studio in Darjeeling. Arthur Pereira, a Fellow of the Royal Photographic Society, agreed to do the processing there. Unprocessed films were sent to him by relays of horsemen.

However, when Mallory and Irving failed to return from their last climb, Noel had a documentary on his hands with no climax. He filled in with shots of Tibetan life and - for more publicity - managed to persuade a party of genuine Buddhist lamas to accompany him to England. There, they danced and blew blasts on their traditional thighbone trumpets,

The Dalai Lama was horrified with these antics, complaining that his priests had been seduced from their normal duties and persuaded to prostitute their art; they had also been illegally smuggled out of the country.

It was ten years before the British were allowed on Everest again. And as for the dancing lamas, they didn't dare go home and remained on the other side of the border.

Photography continued to be Noel's chief passion for the rest of his life though he never returned to Everest. When colour photography made his photographs seem old fashioned, he painstakingly coloured his entire collection. In their seventies, he and his wife (who had been with him in Tibet in 1924) continued to travel and give lectures.

Noel had deep religious beliefs. In 1933, he was present at the canonisation of St Bernadette in St Peters, Rome. He was privileged to sit near the high altar. He had provisioned himself with two - as it turned out - lightly boiled eggs, secreted in his coat-tails. There was rather a mess when he sat down in his pew. He had brought with him a small camera made to look like a prayer book. With this, he secured the only pictures of the service. He lectured widely on the saint and there can be no doubt that he saw in her experience, a divine revelation.

During the Second World War, he worked in intelligence for four years.

John Noel - soldier, revolver expert, mountaineer, photographer, author, lecturer, artist and master craftsman - won praise from everyone who got to know him. Sir Francis Younghusband, former President of the Royal Geographic Society, wrote that 'he was a man of deep intensity of nature and of fine feeling for mountain beauty'; and of his part on the expeditions he went on to say that, whatever the occasion, 'when most wanted Noel would be there. Every member... said on his return that Noel worked harder than anyone.'

John Noel lived in Brenzett, Romney Marsh, Kent, surrounded by reminders of his epic expeditions to Mount Everest. He died there on March 13th 1989, at the age of 99.

Unable to Walk Well...He flew!

JOHN LANKESTER PARKER (1896-1965)

On October 17th, 1916, when John Lankester Parker first appeared on Short Brothers' Kent airstrip as a test pilot, the senior partner, Horace Short, walked off the site. He had argued that Parker was too young (he was 20) and at first had refused to let him fly at all. Parker had then threatened to resign from the company, causing Horace to say that OK if he broke his neck, so be it!

Parker flew all four new bombers that the Rochester based aeronautical engineers had made and were waiting to test. Even Horace had to admit that the young Parker was indeed a very fine pilot - particularly as one of the engines of one of the planes

John Lankester Parker

had failed and he had had to make a forced-landing in a small field. It was in fact said that his handling of aircraft was flawless.

From 1918 until the end of the Second World War, Parker was chief test pilot at Shorts. During this time, he flew every Short prototype. He is also recognised as having been one of the world's greatest flying-boat pilots. And these were the days when test pilots were given the adulation that today is reserved for pop stars.

John Lankester Parker was born on April 11th 1896, at Barton Mills, Suffolk, the second son of a flour miller, Luther Charles Frederick Parker. As a small boy, John suffered from polio. He made a good recovery although it left him with a limp in both legs for the rest of his life.

Naturally, this handicapped him in games at Thetford Grammar School, where he was a pupil.

In 1912, aged 16, he saw his first aeroplane in flight. That was enough - his mind was made up. Flying would be his life - not something so utterly boring as milling flour. But his parents were against a flying career, partly because of the costs involved. An uncle, however, backed the lad and agreed to finance his education. So in 1913, Parker joined the Vickers flying school at Brooklands and in June 1914, he was awarded his Royal Aero Club's Aviation Certificate, number 813.

His disability prevented him from joining the Royal Flying Corps, so he became an instructor at the Hendon Flying School at £1.50 a week. Then, raising £25, he decided to move to Lake Windermere where he could learn to fly seaplanes.

He had an hour's instruction for £10. The machine on which he learnt was called the Waterhen, owned by a Roland Ding. The pupil sat in the rear cockpit and leaned over the instructor to take the controls! Not altogether surprisingly, his first take-off was described as traumatic and his instructor grounded him for ham-fistedness and left to go away for the weekend. This left a lot of disgruntled pupils anxious to continue their lessons. Nothing daunted, Parker took the plane out of its shed and proceeded to give free instruction for an unprecedented 50 flights over the weekend. He even sent one pupil up on a solo flight and awaited Roland Ding's return with some trepidation.

Much to John's surprise, Ding congratulated him on his enterprise and made him an instructor - unpaid. However this did allow Parker to build up his flying hours. The planes were unreliable, under-powered and almost incapable of leaving the water. Parker experimented with different designs of floats and towed them behind a motor boat with a fishing rod and line. In this way he made useful improvements.

Parker was learning to fly but finding it difficult to live. Not being able to afford anything better, he made a packing case in the corner of the hanger his home. He even sold his bicycle so as he could subsist. At the end of three months of this, Ding paid him £1.50 a week. To John's delight, this was soon raised to £6. He taught 75 pupils without a fatality - something of a record for those days.

In 1916, the flying school was taken over by the Admiralty for war purposes. Rear Admiral Murray Sueter asked John if he wanted to be a test pilot and introduced him to his friend, Horace Short. John rode to Eastchurch in Kent to meet Horace, an alarming man, often angry and with a head about twice normal size. But he was also relentless in his pursuit of quality and had remarkable technical ability. He had two younger brothers, who also worked for the company. Short Brothers took Parker on as chief test pilot for a trial period of three months. In the event, he stayed till the 1940s.

In his early years at Shorts, there was insufficient work to keep him fully occupied so he also looked for freelance work. He arranged to fly for an American called Prodger. Routine test flights paid £10; prototypes were negotiable. In this way, he gained wide experience of different planes and could almost tell a plane's flying ability by looking at it.

In January 1918, he had a close brush with death. He was flying a Norman Thompson flying boat over water, when the pusher propeller came off and wrecked the tail. The plane dived into the water, from where Parker was picked up by a minesweeper eight hours later.

His record at Shorts was impressive. He tested all the many aircraft produced by the company. These included the Shirl, the Silver Streak, and a very small experimental flying-boat of some 24-brake horsepower. After these, there were the Singapore, Calcutta, Gurnard, Amphibian, Kent, Sarafand, Scion and the Scion Senior - the Empire Class flying-boats with which Imperial Airways did so much to put British commercial aviation on the map. There were also the planes involved in the start of the regular Atlantic service - the Stirling, Sunderland, Shetland and others. Parker tried them all.

In 1943 Parker was made a director of Short Bros. In 1948, he became the first recipient of the Brackley Memorial Trophy - awarded annually to a British subject ... for the most outstanding achievement in the operation of flying boats.

He was master of the Guild of Air Pilots and Navigators from 1951 to 1953 and voted in again in 1956. In the Guild's newsletter, his obituary describes him as a man having a quiet demeanour, keen brain and modest sense of humour. It also praises his remarkable skill.

He retired from flying in 1958 and became director and chairman of the family milling business of Parker Bros. (Mildenhall) Ltd.

After his death in 1965, the Guild's benevolent fund set out to raise £1000. But so popular had Parker been, more than double this was subscribed. At his memorial service, somebody recalled the way that Parker had dismissed the aftermath of polio which never really left him: 'As I have difficulty in walking', he said then, 'I had better learn to fly.'

* * *

The first woman George Cross

DAPHNE JOAN MARY PEARSON (1911-2000)

Around midnight on May 30th 1940, 29-year-old Corporal Daphne Pearson of the Medical Service was lying on her bunk in the Women's Auxiliary at Detling in Kent. She didn't know it then but she was about to carry out a deed that would make her famous. She was used to the Anson aircraft spluttering a bit when they returned from a raid. She recalled, 'we always had to be ready as there were many prangs among our own aircraft.' But this night - as she lay sleeping

Daphne Pearson

fitfully - she heard something more than a splutter, more, much more than a minor prang. Through the window she saw the Anson, one engine on fire, crash in the middle of the runway.

The Ansons of 500 squadron, Royal Auxiliary Air Force, had taken off earlier from Detling, flown over the enemy coast and had been expected back soon after midnight. One of the aircraft, failing to release its bomb load, headed back to base. Over the Channel, it developed engine trouble. Worse was to come. When it started to line up for landing, the engine burst into flames. Then it started to lose height rapidly. As it crash-landed heavily, it slid across the airfield, the flames rapidly spreading along the fuselage. The bombs had not yet exploded and there were surely only seconds to go before the flames reached them.

In her quarters, Corporal Pearson quickly pulled on her fisherman's jersey, slacks, and Wellingtons, grabbed her tin hat and ran out of the building and across the field. She could see a dull glow where the Anson had finally come to a stop. She scrambled over a hedge, fell down an incline and was stung as she plunged through a bank of nettles. Nearing the wreck, she saw two men carrying another man, who was screaming.

'He's got a broken back,' one of the two supporting men called. 'All right, leave him to me,' Pearson said, 'go and get the fence down for the ambulance.' The two men made their way to the sick quarters. Pearson started to attend to the third man, the pilot, who was groaning in pain. She unclipped his harness and found that his neck was injured and feared he had a broken back. She started to give him first aid when he mumbled that there was a full load of unexploded bombs on board. In response, she quickly dragged him over a ridge and threw herself on top of him to protect him. She removed her own tin hat and put it on the pilot's head.

He muttered something about his face. She saw there was a lot of blood and a tooth sticking out of his jaw. Pearson said afterwards: 'I reassured him about his face, pulled the broken tooth out and was just going to look at his ankle when the plane went up in a tremendous explosion'.

The petrol tank and one of the 120-lb bombs exploded simultaneously. And although they were close to the blast - about 30 yards - the ridge protected them from most of the splinters and debris. If Pearson hadn't moved them, it is unlikely they would have survived. She said later that the air had been sucked from her body and that the air around them 'seemed to collapse'. Other helpers rushing towards them were blown away like leaves in the wind.

As soon as stretcher-bearers took the injured pilot away, Pearson searched the area for other injured survivors. And despite the fact that another bomb could have gone off at any moment, she acted with complete disregard for her own safety.

She returned to the base and was on duty at 8'clock that morning as usual.

The following month she received her commission and in July the *London Gazette* announced that Pearson - now promoted from corporal to Assistant Section Officer - had won the Empire Gallantry Medal on July 19 - the first woman to win a gallantry award during the Second World War. In August, she went to Buckingham Palace for the investiture - 'on a blazing hot day, when nearly all the men fainted and we spent most of the time getting water for them.' Winston Churchill took time off in the Commons to praise her gallantry. On August 3rd, the *Kent Messenger* carried an account of her bravery and printed her picture.

The following year she was at the Palace again to receive the new George Cross in exchange for her Gallantry Medal. The king told her that she was the first woman to win the coveted award. The GC had only been introduced on November 3rd 1942 and is worn above all other medals (except the VC). It is awarded only for acts of the greatest heroism or the most conspicuous courage in circumstances of extreme danger. The inscription says simply: For Gallantry.

Daphne Pearson was born near Christchurch, Hampshire (now Dorset) on May 26th 1911, daughter of the Reverend J H Pearson. After attending St Brandon's Clergy Daughters' School in Bristol, she apprenticed herself to a photographer, G. Methuen Brownlee, a niece of Dr W G Grace, the famous cricketer. For eight years, Pearson worked at the profession with her own studio in St Ives.

Ill health - which dogged her all her life forced her to sell the studio in the mid-1930s. She worked variously as a chauffeur and as manageress of the Ditton Court Farm shop, on the main road going into Maidstone. She lived opposite and her house and the shop remain today.

Her interest in flying began early. While still in her teens, she made regular visits to Ramsgate Civil Airport. She joined the 19th ATS Company attached to the Royal West Kent Regiment. Later, she was one of 15 girls who became the nucleus of the WAAF, attached to 500 Squadron, Kent's own auxiliary squadron. She served at several Bomber Command stations until the end of her service career.

Pearson spent frequent, long periods in hospital, while in the services and in civy street. After the war, she joined the civil service and became an Assistant Governor in the Prison Service. She took evening classes in horticulture and later became assistant to the keeper of the herbarium at the Royal Botanical Gardens at Kew. She subsequently owned a shop in Kew, selling gardening equipment, fresh produce and flowers

She immigrated to Australia in 1959 but returned to Britain almost every year for GC reunions. For many years, she helped a friend run a farm outside Melbourne and made great efforts to have her memoirs published - but was unsuccessful. She died in Australia on July 25th 2000.

* * *

Daphne Pearson

Police Heroes

A Kent policeman's lot can be a difficult one. Every day the men and women of the force put their lives on the line coping with people in trouble or with wrong-doers, many of whom have become increasingly violent. A policeman may have to cope with someone pointing a loaded gun at him, or - as one of the incidents given below illustrates - a gun that looks real but may in fact be a replica. The police have to make a judgment. Do they risk their own lives - and the lives of near-by civilians - just in case the gun may be real? Do they shoot in self-defence? Sadly perhaps, these days guns are getting more common. And - in response - more and more police are having to be armed themselves.

But Kent police aren't just involved with criminals. A policeman may have to help sort out a squabble between neighbours. Or he may be called to the scene of a car accident, where there are those who urgently need hospital. Who was at fault comes later. Police have to be everywhere at all times and always be right. We're disappointed, we get angry, we complain - when we discover that police too are only human.

Below are some of the experiences our police have gone through during the last century. It's a tiny sample of police heroes, who in one way or another deserve our thanks - and quite often, a medal too.

What Shall We Do with a Drunken Sailor?

WALTER HENRY SOUTHEY

It was 11.25pm on November 3rd 1919. Inspector Southey, 48, and PC Leeming were on duty at the Dover Esplanade when they heard a splash - the sound coming from the Wellington Dock. Rushing to the side of the dock, they saw a man struggling in the water. A lifebuoy was thrown to him but he failed to take hold of it.

Without hesitation, Southey threw off his great coat and - ignoring the icy November temperature of the water - jumped into the dock and held the man up while Leeming threw a rope to them. Southey put the rope around the man and the constable tried to pull him out of the water. The weight, however, was too great so the inspector swam with the man to some near-by iron steps, where Leeming helped to hold the man up.

The constable had already blown his whistle for help and three more police now arrived to help pull the man out of the water. He was the worse for drink and suffering from hypothermia, having been in the water so long. He was taken to hospital but it wasn't till the next day that he could identify himself as an able seaman of the destroyer, HMS *Sceptre*.

Man overboard!

EDWIN JOHN POLLINGTON

At about 2.15pm on Sunday July 10th 1927, at Granville Dock, Dover, Charles Powell, one of the crew of the dredger *Gymp,* was crossing the railless gangway from the quayside to the vessel, a distance of about five or six feet. He tripped and fell into the water, striking his head slightly on the side of the ship.

The captain and mate went to Powell's assistance and grasped him over the side of the vessel. However, the man's weight and the force of the water running from the sluice gates close by, forced them to let go. Not only that, but the mate too was pulled into the water.

Just then, PC Edwin John Pollington, who had heard the shouts for help, came running. Seeing that Powell was nearly exhausted, he threw off his tunic and helmet, dived in and was able to keep the man afloat until the dredger's boat came round and all three men were hauled on board.

Powell quickly recovered from his ordeal. Pollington was taken into the Hotel de Paris, where he had a bath. Someone lent him some trousers, which were rather short in the leg. He then went home by tram.

A Major Brush with a Horse & Cart

WILLIAM ALFRED JEBEZ WAIT

Just before 1pm on Monday June 26th 1933, a Mr. Haskings was driving a horse and cart down King Street towards the Market Place, Ramsgate. He swerved to avoid hitting a pedestrian, and turned his trap sharply towards the side of the road. The rear wheel passed over a crate being unpacked by the side of the road, and then bounced on to a handcart. The startled pony plunged forward and the wheel of the trap struck a motor-cycle and sidecar combination.

The trap overturned, throwing Mr. Haskings to the ground in front of a passing car which just managed to stop in time. Mr. Haskings was nevertheless badly shaken and taken to hospital.

In the meantime, with the trap lying on its side, the frightened pony dashed down the street towards the Market Place. The High Street was crowded with pedestrians. The bobby on duty was PC Wait, who dashed forward to intercept the horse and grabbed the reins, which checked the animal's speed. Just as he did so, the cart struck him a heavy blow on the temple and knocked him unconscious. However his plucky action meant that the pony was stopped a few yards further on.

An ambulance was called which took Wait to the Ramsgate General Hospital, where he was found to be suffering from concussion. He was off-duty for 12 months because of his injuries but was rewarded by the Carnegie Hero Trust.

Heroic PC in River Rescue

PC PETER FARRELL (1961-)

Peter Farrell

Some time after 10pm on Wednesday May 15th, 1991, near the Empire Wharf on the River Medway, Chatham, Kent, two men were seen in the water struggling for their lives.

Nicholas Dennis Maile was clinging to an upturned dinghy. The water was extremely cold; he had been in the water for some 20 minutes and he couldn't swim. He had been weakened by the cold and was showing signs of shock. He was in imminent danger of losing his hold on the dinghy and slipping under the water.

A second man, Anthony Estcourt Boucher, was lying on the mud flats on the water's edge and appeared to be choking on his own vomit. Maile called out to a nearby houseboat that Boucher was in the greater danger and should be rescued first.

David James, on board a near by houseboat, saw Boucher and crawled some 30 yards through the mud and secured a line around him. With the assistance of another man on the houseboat, they were able to affect a rescue. Maile, however, was still in the water and in great danger.

A local policeman, PC Peter Farrell, arrived at the scene and immediately stripped off his uniform. He tied a life preserver to a lifeline and set off across the mud at the water's edge. The mud was thick and wet and slippery. Farrell crawled and slithered through the mud on his stomach before reaching the water. He then managed to swim out to the man and brought him ashore.

For these heroic rescues, Farrell was awarded the Chief Constable's Commendation and James the Chief Constable's Certificate of Merit. Both men were additionally awarded the Royal Humane Society's Award and the Silk Cut Special Nautical Award.

Peter Farrell was born in Manchester on July 4th 1961 and was educated at the local Lilly Lane Junior School and Brookdale Park High. On September 13th 1977, he joined the army and spent 11 years in the Irish Guards. Peter has always been something of a sportsman and remembers he won 'lots of things' for running races during his time in the forces.

On July 18th 1988, Peter joined the Kent Police, serving the Medway towns of Chatham, Rochester and Gillingham. He recently moved from his uniformed post to the CID as a Detective Constable. He is a keen diver and has dived at various places around the south coast.

A loaded gun or a machete attack. It's all in a day's work.

PC KEVIN CORBY (1957-) PC JULIAN PEGLER (1960-)

About 5.10 on the evening of January 27th, 1992, in Maison Dieu Road, Dover, a lone gunman brandished his pistol and was just about to reload. Two unarmed policemen, PC Kevin Corby and PC Julian Pegler, had been summoned by a 999 call with a report of two shots. They rushed towards the gunman. What exactly, at that moment, was Kevin Corby thinking?

'There wasn't time to be scared,' he said. Then, like many brave men, he made light of it. 'Any policeman in those circumstances would have acted like I did'. Julian Pegler wasn't frightened either. He only felt excited. Fear came with hindsight.

So what did they do? At first, Corby told the man to drop the gun and the man swore at him. He was heading for the busy town centre and they realised what an armed man might do there. The pistol was pointing upwards. Corby threw his torch at the gunman and missed. Pegler knew they must get to the man before he got to them. The two of them tackled him.

Kevin Corby

Pegler cannoned into him. The man hit Pegler on the side of the head with the pointed end of the pistol. Pegler went down momentarily but then grabbed the man's arm. Corby took hold of the man's other arm and began to struggle. Other police arrived and lent a hand to subdue the man.

There had been no sound of a further gun shot, no sudden pain, no blood. The two policemen had got hold of what was in reality, a replica. The gunman had been lucky. 'It looked realistic enough', Corby said. 'If I'd been armed, I would have shot him.' And armed response police and vehicles had been called for. When Corby told the young gunman how near to death he'd been, the man went white. On May 22nd 1992, the 'gunman' appeared at Maidstone Crown Court and was sent to prison for nine months.

The two constables who initiated the action, Kevin Corby and Julian Pegler, were both awarded the Queen's Commendation for Brave Conduct.

Corby's family is well represented in the police force. He's got a brother in the Cambridge police, a brother-in-law in the Kent police and another brother in the Ministry of Defence force.

As well as being a police marksman, shooting is also a hobby. 'I get paid for something I enjoy', he says. He's a good shot and qualifies with a 90 per cent mark every year. Shooting is also something of a family business. His mother was a crack shot and won a number of prizes.

Corby is often involved in protection work. For example, he may be called to back up the Metropolitan police when someone important and at risk visits Kent.

Corby was born in Folkestone on June 6th 1957, but has always lived in Deal. After attending the Walmer Secondary School, he worked briefly for the post office before making a decision between committing his future to the marines or the police force. (as a boy he was in the Marine

Cadets). He joined the police in 1976 when he was 19 years old and his first posting was Tonbridge. He's had a good career in the police, he says and doesn't plan to retire until he's 49. He is married and he and his wife have a young boy.

Julian Pegler was born in Dover on May 25th 1960. He lived in Capel, went first to Capel Primary School and then to Dover Grammar. Why did he join the police force? He first joined the harbour board police and moved to his present position in 1990. He needed a job and it seemed a good idea at the time. He's never regretted the decision and plans to stay in the force until he is about 55. His main interest outside his work is reading history.

I asked Julian Pegler how dangerous he considered his job. Had he previously had to confront armed violence? Yes. He'd recently had a tussle with a man with a machete. His colleague, PC Gareth Dempster, had come off worst, and had his face slashed open, needing 13 stitches. Pegler was hurt slightly on his hand.

It's a dangerous job being a policeman, I suggested. 'Potentially,' Pegler said quietly. 'You just have to be in the wrong place at the wrong time.'

And as Kevin Corby had said previously, violence is part of a day's work. It's nothing to get excited about.

'To Light a Candle'

LADY SUE RYDER (1923-2000)

Lady Sue Ryder at Travnik in Bosnia

It was her favourite quotation - 'It is better to light one candle than to curse the darkness'- and it was most apt for Sue Ryder. This small, pale, Benenden-educated, intense woman devoted her life to helping the incurably ill. But she would never have recognised herself in the context of this book. A devout convert to Catholicism, she simply believed she was carrying out God's work.

When, in 1978, the letter arrived from No. 10, telling her she had been made a life peer, she put off opening the letter for hours, with the thought, 'Gosh, what have I done now?' And even when she opened the envelope, she thought there must be some mistake - 'a bit of a muddle.' But there was no mistake. In a small way, it was simply a grateful nation saying thank you for a lifetime's heroic work and sacrifice.

Baroness Ryder of Warsaw, was born Sue Ryder on July 3rd 1923, in Leeds, Yorkshire, to a large farm-owning family. Her mother, Mabel, had married widower Charles Ryder in 1911, and the marriage had produced five children.

In addition to their estate at Scarcroft, the family had a second estate at The Hall, Great Thurlow in Suffolk, where they spent the summer months. In the 1930s, they sold the Yorkshire estate and lived full-time at Thurlow.

As a child, Sue had seen the terrible conditions of the slum-dwellers - who lived 'almost walking distance' from their estate. Her mother, who invited these desperately poor children over to play in the estate's fields, was a campaigner for slum clearance and improved living conditions. She perhaps laid down the path along which her daughter was to travel.

At the age of 12, Sue was sent to what was then, the comparatively new school of Benenden in Kent. The school grew rapidly from 24 pupils in her first autumn term to 126 a year later. Sue remembered the school policy of 'freedom within the law', which made the girls feel trusted and responsible. Years later, she wrote to one of the founders, a Miss Bird (known as Birdie), to ask about the beginnings of the school and the philosophy it wished to impart to its girls. Her reply seems so apposite to the life lived by Sue Ryder that it deserves to be quoted.

'We wanted the school to be a normal, friendly, happy place where learning to live life as a whole went side by side with academic training. We hoped that you would all find a philosophy which would help you in meeting difficulty, trouble and opportunity, and that in planning your lives you would always be aware of the needs of others and serve them with compassion and understanding...'

Looking into the future, Sue wondered if she would become a nurse - one of her brothers was a doctor - but was afraid that she mightn't be able to cope. She showed an active interest in the world outside the school. She remembers feeling depressed about the needless slaughter of the Spanish Civil War, and admired the way George V1 and Queen Elizabeth reacted to their sudden obligation to take the throne.

She also became aware of the 'Jewish problem' and British government policy that meant 'no admission without financial guarantee'. Although a pupil in a lower class, she was allowed to attend history lessons in the sixth form and became more aware of the long history of rejection suffered by the Jews. She learnt too of some of the objectives of Adolf Hitler. At the beginning of the Second World War, she saw the map of Europe redrawn by the Nazis showing which countries (including Britain) that they aimed to conquer. For a young schoolgirl, she seemed to know a great deal about the world and the threat from Germany.

In her autobiography, *Child of my Love,* the future Baroness Ryder of Warsaw writes bitterly about the way - as she saw it - that Britain let down the Poles in not giving assistance and arms to help defend the country more effectively against the German onslaught. Poles on horseback pathetically confronted German tanks.

When war broke out, Sue was still a 16-year-old schoolgirl. The family took in evacuees from the slums and Sue left school and donned a nurse's uniform to work in a hospital. There was some simple training and examinations that she subsequently passed.

She joined the First Aid Nursing Yeomanry (FANY), which had been originally been set up in 1907. She also 'cooked' her real age and joined the Special Occupations Executive (SOE) and signed the Official Secrets Act. The SOE carried out a campaign of harassment and sabotage in occupied Europe and later in the Far East. As part of her training, Sue was taught the rudiments of the Czech and Polish languages but never became fluent in either. She was posted briefly with the Czech section but found herself more and more involved with Poland and carried out a number of highly secret and dangerous missions.

The information carried was vital to the war effort, and a message - destined for the Polish Commander-in-Chief in London - could include the following information:- U-Boats in the Baltic; German troop movements; V1 and V2; Auschwitz; Photographs for forged documents; Escape routes; German industry; Munitions factories; Sabotage; Information and plans of enemy aircraft and armour; the Jewish ghettos and the rising in the Warsaw ghetto; co-operation with the Resistance in Hungary and Germany; extermination of Poles and Jews, particularly in the parts annexed to the Reich.

The couriers - all operatives were known as the 'bods' - were not, however, allowed to know the exact nature of the information they carried, in case they were captured and tortured. A third of the women sent to France during the Second World War never returned. As women, they certainly got no preferential treatment in the hands of the Germans and were not treated as prisoners-of-war. A usual method of disposing of such agents was to give them a lethal injection and then shove them into the ovens. The gruesome truth was that many were burned alive before the fatal drug began to work.

Sue joined the Polish section of the SOE, where she was profoundly impressed by the optimism and sense of sacrifice exhibited by the Polish 'bods'. She began to think of ways in which their faith, courage and humour might be perpetuated. In 1942, she volunteered to do relief work in Poland and elsewhere, when she could be released from SOE duties

In 1943, she went with one of the Special Duties Squadrons to North Africa and later to Italy. Winters on the continent - especially during the winter of 1943 - could be intensely cold, with temperatures down to twenty-degrees-below-freezing or lower. Blizzards were blinding and the diesel in the trucks froze. In Naples, a typhus epidemic raged, caused by the appalling conditions, from which many of the local population died.

As a member of the SOE, Sue had known about many of the Nazi atrocities but it wasn't until the allied advance, when the death camps were being opened up, that the true horror of German-occupied Europe came to light. It was this suffering particularly in Poland, that confirmed Sue Ryder's lifetime desire to bring help wherever and whenever she could.

In 1945, she went with relief units caring for survivors of bombed-out

France, nursing the sick and helping dig bodies from the ruins. She started prison visiting as a member of Amis Volontaires Francais (AVF) - in France and Germany. She kept detailed records of all the prisoners she saw, whom she referred to as her 'Boys'. Most were young Poles. Going through the papers of those in German prisons, she saw that many were far away from their families and that if she didn't visit them, nobody would.

She drew attention to prisoners-of-war - of many nationalities - who were held in German prisons. Some had been convicted for stealing food in places where there were extreme food shortages. She found work for former prisoners and tried to make contact with their families. She also brought many survivors of the concentration camps to a holiday in Britain. It was for her work with prisoners in Germany that she was awarded the OBE in 1957, at the age of 34.

Few things were able to defeat her. She was instructed to collect a lorry in London and load it with stoves and drugs, for the treatment of tuberculosis and typhus. On her way out of London, on the Vauxhall Bridge Road, the lorry broke down. Enlisting the help of passers-by, she got the vehicle into the gutter, analysed the problem and proceeded to clean the carburettor and the petrol pump and replace the spark plugs, then proceeded on her way.

After her work on the continent, she returned to England, determined to bring relief to those who had suffered so terribly in the war. She writes of wanting to provide a 'living memorial'. In 1953, Sue established the Sue Ryder Foundation in Suffolk, with the help of a small legacy, credit from her bank, and much optimism. She bought her mother's house, which was to become both the headquarters of the Foundation and a Home for physically handicapped people.

In February 1955, Leonard Cheshire - famous for the many Cheshire Homes for those handicapped by war - invited Sue to see his new Home at Ampthill, in Bedfordshire. She travelled to the house but very nearly missed meeting the war hero commander of the famous 617 Squadron - and her future husband. She tried to enter by the wrong gate, found it locked and was about to return home - she was suffering from a kidney infection and it was a cold, bleak day. Luckily for their future happiness, she changed her mind, found the right gate and announced herself.

For both of them, it was a voyage of discovery. Neither knew of the other's work and as they chatted, they wanted to know more about each other. There were differences in the way the Homes worked. The Cheshire Homes were intended mainly for the physically handicapped, including the young. The Ryder Foundation cares for the sick and handicapped of all age groups and specialises in patients diagnosed with cancer, Huntingdon's Disease and other neurological illnesses; in addition, the Foundation operated a Holiday Scheme for survivors of the Gestapo prisons, Nazi concentration camps and Soviet labour camps.

Leonard talked about his work and showed her over the Home. Sue told him about the aims of her 'living memorial'. When she left, Leonard Cheshire confided to others: 'I could not define it, but [meeting Sue Ryder] made a vivid impression on me.'

After this, they met at intervals - in Leicestershire and on many shared drives to the continent. They co-operated in each other's work and subsequently, Sue became a trustee of the Cheshire Homes and Leonard a the councillor of the Sue Ryder Foundation.

But, as Sue says, 'it was in India that [they] really got to know each other.' In 1957, she flew from Moscow to Delhi, to be met by Leonard at the airport. They then travelled to various parts of the country by train and bus and founded the Ryder-Cheshire Mission for the relief of suffering. They also visited a number of local Cheshire Homes. Leonard had set them up but they were run and supported by local Indians. Along the way they were warmly welcomed by friends who, almost invariably, put them up for the night.

In the following February, they became engaged. Sue describes how carefully she thought about this and vowed that nothing - including marriage - would interfere with the work that was her life. They sent a jointly-signed letter to all their friends, supporters and colleagues, asking for their blessings. The wedding ceremony took place in a private chapel in Bombay on April 9th 1959. Their son, Jeromy, was born in 1960, and daughter, Elizabeth, in 1962.

Shortly after their wedding, they responded to a number of invitations from Australia and New Zealand, to speak about their work. It was a heavy schedule - Sue gave as many as nine talks a day. Their visit also led to the establishment of a number of Ryder-Cheshire Foundation Homes

Back in Europe, Sue felt drawn back to the country she felt closest to. She wrote: 'I feel I belong to Poland.' By the time of her death, she had established 28 Sue Ryder Homes in that country. Most of the materials came from Britain but the Polish authorities ran the Homes and provided the staff. She drove thousands of miles to and from Poland, her lorry loaded up with medical supplies, food and other comforts.

But she never forgot other commitments, including to Yugoslavia, one of the countries SOE had trained her for, back in the war years. She set up 22 Homes in Yugoslavia, some of which were damaged in the Bosnian war. Both Yugoslavia and Poland remembered their benefactor by showering her with honours.

Sue Ryder was appointed CMG in 1976, and created a life peer as Baroness Ryder of Warsaw in 1979. Poland was so important to her that she insisted, unconventionally, on associating her peerage with Warsaw - usually only service chiefs are accorded this kind of privilege.

By the 1980s, Britain had six Sue Ryder Homes, providing continuing care for some 900 patients. They had many imaginative fund raising ideas, including a Wellington Boot throwing contest and the 'fastest bed-maker in town' competition.

Sue Ryder had achieved a very great deal. For one woman to achieve such overwhelming success in so many places required an unremitting dedication and a Herculean appetite for hard work. Sue was not easy to work for - she set high standards and expected others to follow. Had she been more congenial, perhaps she would not have achieved so much. Her working day began shortly after 4.30am and lasted until late. She also found it difficult to delegate, wanting to stay in control of everything - but her personal concern for everybody in her care was genuine. She lived frugally, never drawing a salary and dressing in clothing bought from her charity shops. Her home was a flat in the Foundation's headquarters.

It is clear from her writing that her husband meant a great deal to her and that they shared many beliefs. Chief among these was their great faith but also their patriotism. They loved their country, the Commonwealth, and its monarchy and believed that Britain should set a moral example to the world.

They shared each other's problems in the brief time they had together - even their mealtimes were interrupted by incessant telephone calls. But Leonard was the weaker of the two. He didn't always feel physically strong, had serious health problems and ignored pleas from his doctor to cut down on his punishing schedule

By the summer of 1991, Leonard was diagnosed as suffering from tuberculosis, coeliac disease, and skin cancer, and in February 1992, with motor neurone disease. He died from heart failure on July 31st 1992, when Sue received letters of condolence from all over the world, including from the Queen and the then prime minister, John Major.

After her husband's death, Sue continued to play a significant role in her charity until 1998, when she agreed to relinquish her role as the Foundation trustee on her 75th birthday. The Foundation was given a new name, Sue Ryder Care. However, Sue didn't like the way the new bosses of

Lady Sue Ryder and her husband, Leonard Cheshire

the Foundation were operating and in response, she launched the Bouverie Foundation. By the end of the century, the new charity was going well and working on humanitarian projects in France, Poland, and Italy.

But even Sue's indomitable spirit couldn't last forever and she died, after being ill with cancer for two years, on November 8th 2000, aged 77. A memorial service was held at St Peters Church, Little Thurlow, near Haverhill. The former Bishop of Chelmsford, Ipswich and St Edmundsbury, the Rt Rev John Waine, chosen for his work as a patron of the Sue Ryder Foundation, led the tributes. 'She gave so much', he said. 'She was a remarkable lady whose passion, dedication, and faith were nothing less than double strength...'

* * *

The Renaissance Man, in Whom we do Delight

SIDNEY, SIR PHILIP, (1554-1586)

Seldom has a man been so honoured in his passing. 'Farewell the worthiest knight that lived...farewell the friend, beloved of all, that had'st no foe but chance.' So went the cries of the multitudes that thronged the streets of London as the cortège of Philip Sidney passed slowly by. The great men of Elizabethan England lived in a grand and ostentatious manner and they expected their funerals to follow suite. But seldom was a mere knight buried so grandly nor with such genuine affection from lords and commoners alike.

Philip Sidney may not have been a peer of the realm but his family connections served him as well in death as they had in life. His father-in-law, Sir

Sir Philip Sidney

Francis Walsingham, was one of the great men of the Virgin Queen's court and it was said he 'spared not any cost to have this funeral well performed.' In fact, the funeral had been delayed for four months until Walsingham could raise the funds to finance it.

The procession wound it way through the streets of London, from the Minories Church, where the body had lain in state, to St Paul's, and the people of the city - in their thousands - showed their respect. The streets were so thronged with mourners that there was scarcely enough room for the procession to pass. The houses along the route were full and 'there were few or none that did not shed some tears as the corpse passed by.' The mourning was widespread and more than 200 elegies were written in Philip's memory.

Who was this man whose demise caused such universal distress? Philip Sidney is traditionally hailed as the Elizabethan's 'complete man'. He charmed everybody he met, including kings and princes and great statesmen. There were, however, limits to his achievements. He was a courtier, though at times out of favour with Queen Elizabeth. He was a poet, though unpublished in his lifetime and a soldier who fought just one skirmish, in which he met his death.

Philip was born at Penshurst - the stately Kent manor that is still the home of the Sidney family - on November 30, 1554. He was the eldest son of Sir Henry Sidney by his wife, Mary, daughter of John Dudley, duke of Northumberland. The manor of Penshurst had been given by Edward VI to Philip's father.

There is a famous tree in the gardens of Penshurst that was traditionally believed to have been planted on the day of Philip Sidney's birth - and Ben Jonson's poem celebrates this:

Of a nut was sent,

At his great birth, where all the Muses met

Today, improved dating methods reckon the tree to be over 1000 years old. However, it is in a poor condition and an attempt is being made to clone it.

Philip was well connected, both at home and abroad. He was named after his godfather, Philip II of Spain, Queen Mary's husband. His other godfather was John Russell, first earl of Bedford. His godmother was his widowed grandmother, Jane, duchess of Northumberland. When he was merely nine and a half, his father, then lord president of Wales, appointed him rector of the church of Whitford, Flintshire, a position that yielded him an income of £60 a year - a sum that proved to be a great help in future years when Philip was often short of money. It is believed that the previous incumbent was deprived of the position because of his Catholic leanings. An administrator was appointed to carry out the necessary duties until Philip came of age.

When Philip reached school age, his father, then living at Ludow Castle, found Shrewsbury School convenient, so the lad was sent there. On the day of his arrival, November 16, 1564, another boy joined the school, Fulke Greville, who became a lifelong friend. Greville later wrote '...though I lived with him and knew him from a child yet I never knew him other than a man with such staidness of mind, lovely and familiar gravity, as carried grace and reverence above greater years; his talk ever of knowledge, and his very play tending to enrich his mind, so that even his teachers found something in him to observe and learn above that which they had usually read or taught...'

From an early age, Philip took easily to learning and was only 11 when he wrote letters to his father in both French and Latin. In 1568, he left

Shrewsbury for Christ Church, Oxford, where his circle of admirers continued to grow. His tutor, Thomas Thornton, left directions that the fact that Philip had been his pupil should be recorded on his tombstone. But Philip's health was seldom strong and his uncle, Leicester, who was chancellor of the university, wrote soliciting a licence to eat meat during Lent on behalf of 'my boy Philip Sidney, who is somewhat subject to sickness.'

Philip could count many of the great and the good among his friends. William Cecil, the Queen's chief minister, loved him as a son. Ben Jonson revered him and - as we have already seen - wrote a poem about Philip and Penshurst. Hakluyt, famous for his chronicling the voyages of the Elizabethan seamen, and Camden, the antiquary whose *Britannia* was published in the year of Philip's death - all these were among his closest intimates.

In 1571, Philip was forced to leave Oxford because of the plague and in fact he never took a degree. A year later, Queen Elizabeth granted the lad a licence to travel abroad for two years.

On Philip's Grand Tour of Europe, monarchs, scholars, and the great men of Europe were added to his list of friends. The king of France, Charles IX, bestowed on him the title of Baron and appointed him Gentleman of the Royal Bed Chamber. The Venetian public gave him the freedom of its dominions. And in Poland, he was actually offered the crown!

Perhaps one of Philip's most significant meetings was with the 54-year-old Hubert Languet, learned protestant and controversialist; he struck up a friendship with Philip and became almost a father figure to the young man. He persuaded Philip to have his portrait painted and Veronese was the artist chosen. The painting - now sadly lost - was left in Languet's keeping and apparently shows an extremely handsome young man in the bloom of youth. Many of Languet's letters to Philip have survived and in some of these he goes into raptures about the portrait: '...it [the painting] struck me as so beautiful and to resemble you so strongly, that I value nothing else I own more highly...'

It seems likely that this was the same portrait that the poet and diplomat Daniel Rogers, also saw and he too heaps on the praises:...'Well then (may Divine Youth long encircle with soft down those cheeks wherein it resides), who painted you, o Sidney in such a unique manner, and who spread this rosy charm lightly upon your face..' Adulation continues to be heaped on praise.

Early in March 1575, Philip received a summons to return home, amid rumours that he had become a catholic. In fact, Philip was - and remained - a devout protestant and worked strenuously for the protestant cause. Hubert Languet now wrote to his family in England, proving that the accusations against Philip were nonsense. Nevertheless, Philip made his way home.

Back in England, he was obliged to defend his father's administration in Ireland against criticism. (his father had been three times lord deputy governor of Ireland). More daringly, Philip wrote strongly against the proposed marriage of the Queen to the French King's brother, the Duke of Anjou. Following this, he found himself out of favour with Elizabeth and left court left under a cloud. He retired to live with his younger sister, Mary, countess of Pembroke, at her house in Wilton.

It was here - and later at Penshurst - that he began to earn a reputation as a man of letters and some of his work has been compared to that of Shakespeare and Spenser. Perhaps his most important writing can be found in *Arcadia,* described by *The Oxford Companion to English Literature* as 'a prose romance with poems and pastoral eclogues in a wide variety of verse forms'. His other works include *Defence of Poetry, The Lady of May,* and *Astrophel and Stella.* There seems little doubt that his fictional Stella was Penelope Devereux, a girl he first met when she was only 12. At one time, it was thought that he would marry Penelope (and it was her father's dying wish that he should).

The situation, however, was rather complicated. In the circles in which Philip moved, marriages were arranged more for status and financial gain and little consideration was given to 'love' between the couples. Marriage was a powerful political tool for all the rulers of Europe. It could strengthen friendships and even prevent war. Penelope's father, the Duke of Essex, dying of dysentery in Ireland, was known to be in grave financial difficulties, so much so that his promised legacy of £2000 to his daughter was in great doubt. In the end, the idea of their marriage simply faded away. They both married other people - Penelope to Lord Rich and Philip to Frances, daughter of Sir Francis Walsingham. Nothing more is heard of any relationship between Philip and Penelope.

This 'complete man' however, had for long been anxious to prove himself in battle and the opportunity arose in 1586, when he was 32. He was given a command in the Netherlands in an action against the Spanish held town of Zutphen. In his speech to his men before the battle, there are echoes of Shakespeare's *Henry V.* But instead of 'God for Harry, England and St George!', Philip declared that the battle was in God's cause, that they fought for her Majesty, whom they knew so well to be good unto them...against ...men of false religion...enemies to God and his church against Antichrist...'.

But Philip Sidney was no Henry V and in the course of the battle, he did what turned out to be his undoing. Seeing that his fellow-in-arms, Sir William Pelham, lacked thigh armour (cuisses) Philip - baffling as it may seem - took off his own as a mark of solidarity. In consequence of this, leaving himself open to attack, he was mortally wounded. At least this is how the story has been retold - and it was followed by another action that could quite possibly be myth. As he was being carried away from the battle, his loss of blood causing a raging thirst, he refused the cup of water offered to him, pointing to another wounded soldier with the words that have rung down through the pages of history: 'his need is greater than mine'.

Philip received his wound on September 22 and lingered for some weeks, suffering agonies from the primitive attempts by surgeons to remove the bullet. He finally died on October 17, probably of septicaemia.

Sir Philip Sidney, one of the Elizabethan world's most illustrious heroes, was finally laid to rest in St Paul's, in the city of London. His body is no longer there, however, as his remains, along with the rest of the old church, were destroyed in the Great Fire of London in September 1666.

Of the 200 or more elegies that were written in Philip's memory, a few lines from Greville are typical:

Knowledge her light hath lost;
Valour hath slain her knight.
Sidney is dead;
dead is my friend;
dead is the world's delight.

* * *

The First British Woman to Conquer Mt Everest

REBECCA STEPHENS (1961-)

Rebecca Stephens climbing Mt. Everest in 1993

Like most heroes, Rebecca Stephens reached the top of the world simply by overcoming fear, by beating the real terror of the sheer 1,000-feet drops she passed on her way to becoming the first British woman to climb Mount Everest's 29,028 feet. The secret of a true hero is not the bravado of a James Bond but the quality of rising above it all and getting the job done.

And she brought these same qualities to be the first British woman to climb the 'seven summits' - the highest mountain on each of the world's seven continents. Why does she do it? Of course it is a challenge she loves. It makes her feel great, the views are breathtaking, and it enables her to share a particular kind of real passion with her fellow mountaineers. Her achievements were the realisation of a dream. The final ascent on Everest was also a relief. And, as she says towards the end of her autobiographical *Top of the World,* 'life doesn't get much more exciting than this!'

Rebecca Stephens was born on October 3, 1961, at Kemsing, Kent, on the edge of the North Downs. Years later, she remembered thinking how much nicer the hills would have been if, instead of chalk, they had been solid, brown rock, that she could have climbed.

She went to school at St John's Primary School, Sevenoaks, then at the

Tonbridge Grammar School for Girls. She spent a term at the Herriot Watt University in Edinburgh doing Landscape Architecture, changed her mind, and took Agriculture at London University's Wye College, from where she graduated with a BSc in 1983, aged 21.

Setting her sights on being a journalist - and having just graduated in Agriculture - she joined *Farm Business* magazine for a couple of years before the publishers went into liquidation. Anxious to get another job quickly, she became a writer with a magazine called *Communications,* an experience she describes as a 'living nightmare'.

After three months, she landed a job with the Financial Times magazine, *Residents Abroad.* This was much more to her taste and she stayed six years 'travelling all over the world' and ended up as deputy editor. Then a series of events took place to change her life forever.

Rebecca remembers 'a routine morning in the office some time in 1987.' She read a small advertisement in *The Times* about an expedition to the Himalayan mountain, K2, inviting trekkers to ski to the Base Camp. She admits: 'I could have no more located K2 on a map than I could some little known peak in deepest Switzerland'. However, she attended a press conference put on by the Ski Club of Great Britain and met a climber by the name Roger Mear. She had spent some six weeks skiing in the Alps over recent years - but to go on this expedition, she also needed £2,500. Could she go as a journalist and cover the expedition, she asked? Yes, but she needed a sponsor - and try as she might, K2 was not sufficient bait to tempt one.

About two years later, in the summer of 1989, Roger Mear rang again, to invite her to cover an expedition to Mount Everest, as a journalist. Without hesitation, without even thinking, she answered, 'yes, she'd love to'. This time sponsorship came more easily - perhaps it was the magic name of the world's highest mountain. Her parent newspaper, *The Financial Times,* asked her to write a series of articles on the climb - and away she went to join an Anglo-American expedition to scale the still unclimbed North-East ridge of Everest, in Tibet.

The intention was that she would go as far as the Base Camp but in the end decided to go on to Camp One, at a height of some 23,500 feet. She borrowed the kit from a Sherpa and, on a fixed rope, climbed onto the North-East ridge. Her first real climb on a real mountain. And how did she feel? 'Knackered!'

This, however, was the start of something new. She might have been exhausted but, at the same time, she had never felt better in her life. She was surrounded by some of the most extraordinary people she had ever met, from all over the world. Here indeed was real passion - excitement and adventure she had never known. 'The seed was sown,' she told me. It was September 1989, she was 27 years of age and on the edge of a new adventure.

She now said goodbye to scuba-diving in the Maldives, bicycling in China, and hang-gliding in Wales - and headed for the hills. In the early summer of 1990, she climbed Mont Blanc - that she thought to be Europe's highest - only to be told that there was a mountain in the Caucasus called Elbrus that was 3,000 feet higher. Well, she would climb that later.

Nevertheless, Mont Blanc taught her a lot. She learned to bivouac in the snow with just a sleeping bag and a Gore-Tex shell; about cooking over a camp stove; about climbing roped, six in a line, up gullies, over high expansive glaciers and along ridges; and about jumping off ridges and to catch a fall should one of those roped topple off.

Her love affair with mountains deepened. She discovered the wonder of the snowy playground that was the Alps. To wake early, before the sun was up and set off in a line, head torches burning. To watch the moon shadows across the glacier. And to savour the final reward - to stand on the mountain's domed summit at the break of day with - seemingly - all of Europe spread out below.

After Ben Nevis was ticked off the list, she decided on some serious climbing. Kenya was next and she ascended the Diamond Couloir, an ice route on Mount Kenya. The next year, 1991, it was Kilimanjaro.

About this time, she describes a certain feeling of conceit. She still hadn't mastered an overhang, climbed a north face or climbed solo. But, repeatedly, she had escaped the effects of altitude. Never a serious headache, or feeling nausea, or loss of appetite - that others complained of. And there came just the hope that she could climb the world's highest mountain.

But before Everest, there was McKinley in Alaska. Her party - there were four of them that eventually reached the summit - had to wait weeks in a snowhole about 14,000 feet up on the mountain, until the temperature rose and the wind dropped. The wait in itself was another achievement. At last the weather improved enough for them to climb, and on to the summit, Alaska stretched out before them. Her confidence was increasing with every climb.

In the spring of 1993, Rebecca and a team of other climbers set out to make her dream come true. At last she was ready to attempt the climb to the top of Everest. Various firms had given enough sponsorship for the expedition to get under way. She had given up her job and she was now on her own. On the morning of March 11, she fell, exhausted, onto the plane. Destination, Kathmandu.

The climbing party were ten climbers, plus eight Sherpas who would carry the packs and prepare the meals.

How did she feel now that the climb was under way? Put simply, she was ready. She had made all her preparation and hoped she was fit enough for anything that might come. And when she saw other deaths - as she had during her various climbs - how did that affect her? She remembered that around the time she climbed McKinley, 13 had died. But somehow - she wasn't being callous - it didn't connect. 'It was like watching the news on television', she told me. But it also, 'injected her with caution.'

The weather on the way to Everest was hard to take. The nights were freezing but scorching daytime temperatures on the mountain could be as high as 130 degrees Fahrenheit. As they climbed higher and higher, she described the team's own personal condition deteriorating a little at a time - they became thinner, weaker, and their minds fuzzier.

But finally, with the aid of oxygen, they reached the summit. This is how Rebecca describes the final push: 'There was an air of confidence among us now and despite fatigue, thin air, the effort to put one foot in front of the other, and the implausibility of us climbing together on the summit ridge of this, Everest, the most majestic mountain of them all, we knew now that we would make it to the summit. And we knew the moment we were about to arrive, for there, ahead, was the highest bump of them all with lots of flags on top. We stood and waited until the three of us were huddled together in a little cluster, and together stepped on top of the world. It wasn't very dramatic but the joy on the [accompanying] Sherpas' faces made my heart near burst: Summit, summit, summit. We made summit!'

But, with Everest accomplished, there were more mountains to conquer. She had set herself the task of completing her climbing of the rest of the 'Seven Summits' - the highest mountain on each of the seven continents. And she was to do it all in under a year in 1994. She remembered her sponsor's frank statement: 'There is no money unless you're first.' So she completed the rest of the seven in some five months.

The next was Mount Elbrus, in the Caucasus, in Russia - the highest mountain in Europe. After that, it was the beautiful Carstensz in Irian Jaya Pyramid - part of Indonesia. To get there, she walked for a week. After this, she travelled to the South American Andes to climb Mount

Aconagua, the second highest mountain in the world. Then finally, Mount Vinson in Antarctica, where the air was 'sweet and energising', and the extremes of cold among the worst on the planet.

And what does Rebecca do when she's not climbing mountains and raising sponsorship money? Well, she still writes of course, freelancing. She is a trustee for Edmund Hilary's Himalayan Trust. She leads treks in the Himalayas. And she's also joined the lucrative lecture circuit, telling everyone everywhere about the joys of the climb.

There are few better people better able to tell it as it is.

Rebecca Stephens can be reached on 0207-736 1483 or on rebecca.stephens@virgin.net

Rebecca Stephens on Mt. Everest

Sturt's Battle with the Hawkhurst Gang - the Facts Behind the Legend

WILLIAM STURT (1718-1797)

Around five o'clock in the afternoon of April 21, 1747, a battle took place in the pretty Kent village of Goudhurst, between some 150 smugglers of the notorious Hawkhurst Gang and the village militia, headed by the so-called General Sturt. Three smugglers were shot dead and others taken prisoner - giving victory to the militia.

This, and a very great deal more, is the stuff of popular legend, virtually unchallenged until a local sleuth, Tom Browning, painstakingly went through a host of primary sources, to try to discover the truth behind the myth.

Before revealing the results of these researches, it would be helpful to give some idea of the situation in Kent and Sussex during the first half of the eighteenth century. Smuggling was rife and involved not only ruthless ruffians like those of the Hawkhurst Gang but respectable members of society. There is much truth in Kipling's ditty with its line 'brandy for the parson, baccy for the clerk' Even a man of the cloth appreciated a cut price on his favourite tipple and a respected official a duty-free smoke. And even if it was illegal, well everyone did it... It is said, in fact, that smugglers were even financed by wealthy businessmen and the gentry.

The Wealden town of Hawkhurst, from which the gang got its name, was situated near several inland waterways, which the smugglers used for their illegal trade. A lot of it was also horse-packed and sent up to London. In one way or another, the surrounding districts were at high risk from the outlaws. Goudhurst, scene of the famous 'battle', is about four miles from Hawkhurst.

Virtually unchanged today after two and a half centuries, and still with its own duck pond, Goudhurst is situated on a high hill with panoramic views over the surrounding countryside. The gang met at the village house of Spyways, from where they could instantly spot any approach by the authorities. There was also, reputedly, an underground tunnel connecting the lovely old church of St Mary's with the pub, Ye Olde Starre & Crowne (now the Star and Eagle), where the gang stowed its contraband.

The Hawkhurst Gang had for years roamed the south-east of England with impunity and were not adverse to murder and torture if somebody stood in their way. By 1740, their territory stretched over Kent, Surrey and Sussex, from Dover in the east to Brighton in the west, as well as many of the roads that linked London to the coast. There was no police force at this time and customs men with military back-up were spread too thin on the ground to be really effective. And even if gang members were brought to court, some magistrates were too afraid of retribution to risk sending the men to the gallows.

There was a time in the past when the gang would have been satisfied to smuggle on a small scale. But as tariffs rose, their business expanded and rewards became greater. To avoid capture, they armed themselves with a range of firearms and became even more of a force to be reckoned with.

In the months leading up to the famous, often retold, 'battle' in Goudhurst, legend has it that the village had long been terrorised by the Hawkhurst Gang, leaving the villagers too frightened to go out of their houses, even in daytime. Local horses, with or without the owners' permission, were used to ferry illegal goods around the district and residents were woken in the middle of the night with violent demands for food, money, or both.

At the time of our story, it is reported that the Hawkhurst Gang issued a chilling threat that they would slaughter every man, woman and child in Goudhurst, torch the houses and raze the village to the ground - if the locals even thought of challenging their authority. Browning, however, points out that there is no evidence that Goudhurst was in fact terrorised. If there were threats, it was probably mainly bravado. The gang could hardly have intended to really raze the entire village to the ground as it is believed that some of the smugglers, as well as sympathisers, were actually residents of Goudhurst.

But terrorised or not, it seems a clear fact that a local militia was formed to protect the village and that its leader was a local man called William Sturt, who was given the honorary title of General. The articles of association were signed on Friday, April 17th, 1747. Sturt had recently served in Major General Henry Harrison's Regiment of Foot, from which he had received an honourable discharge.

When the Hawkhurst gang heard of the newly formed militia, they managed to capture one of its members and, under torture, forced him to tell them of the militia's intentions. The gang then released him after making him swear that he would not fight against them. He was given a message for General Sturt - total destruction of the village of Goudhurst and everybody in it. The outlaws would gather together a force of over a hundred smugglers. And so confident were they of success that they even named the day when they would take the action.

Thus warned, Sturt and his militia made their preparations. The story has it that trenches were dug, two hundredweight of gunpowder was procured, musket balls were manufactured and firearms cleaned and made ready for use. Barricades were erected and both villagers and militiamen positioned themselves in the church tower and in houses on either side of the main street, with the best marksmen at the windows and on the church tower. The women and children were sent out of town.

The smugglers were on time, almost to the minute, and came galloping into town, each stripped to his shirtsleeves with a handkerchief around his head. They carried carbines, pistols and other weapons. They were led by a ruffian named Thomas Kingsmill, accompanied by his brother George, and the leader proclaimed their bloody intentions in a loud voice. They had recently killed some 50 of His Majesty's officers and soldiers, he called out, and now promised the same fate for the people of Goudhurst. He would broil their hearts and eat them for his supper.

Sturt ordered his men to allow the smugglers to fire first so that his militia would then be acting in self-defence. The Hawkhurst gang fired without effect. The consequent action was published on the centenary of

The Star and Crown (now Star and Eagle) Goudhurst, where George Kingsmill was reputedly killed as he attempted to break down the door at the start of the Battle of Goudhurst

the battle in the *Maidstone Journal, Kentish Advertiser, and South Eastern Intelligence* on April 27th, 1847, as follows: George Kingsmill 'commenced the attack by riding to the Star and Crown Inn door...rearing his horse against it to force it in, when a person from an upper window fired and knocked him from his horse lifeless.' The same paper went on to say, 'another desperate ruffian, named Barnet Woollett, while leaping his horse over the churchyard fence, exclaiming 'shoot and be ——-' was shot dead from the church tower.'

The militia, with the advantage of surprise and having chosen their positions, kept the upper hand and suffered no casualties. The length of the battle was not recorded but after three smugglers had been killed and several wounded, the outlaws fled with the militia in hot pursuit. Some half dozen were rounded up, tried and hanged. Browning points out that there is no evidence for this although another source relates that Thomas Kingsmill and his crony, William Fairall were executed on April 26th, 1749, and their bodies left to hang in chains until the flesh rotted.

But what really happened during that famous Goudhurst battle? There are two short contemporary accounts that probably come as close to the facts of the matter as we are likely to get. But even here, there are discrepancies. The first is from a contemporary issue of the *Gentlemen's Magazine,* for April 1747. The entry is as follows:

'Two smugglers, George Kingsman, and Barnet Wollit, both outlaws the first of which formerly kill'd a man of Hurst Green, were killed in a skirmish with the townsmen of Goudhurst in Kent, who found it necessary to arm against these desperadoes who rob and plunder and live upon the spoil, wherever they come.'

Now a short extract from a letter written to the *Kentish Post* on the day following the battle, April 22nd 1747:

> 'Yesterday, about Five o'clock in the afternoon, 15 smugglers went to Goudhurst, all armed with pistols etc. and swore they would fire the town. The people, having notice of it, got all armed and received their first fire, but none were hurt; they fir'd at the smugglers, and shot two through their heads, whereupon the others made off. The two men kill'd are George Kingsman, an outlaw, who shot a man at Hurst Green some time ago; the other's name is Barnitt Wollitt, an outlaw also. They rob and plunder everybody they meet with.'

But what more is known of the hero of the hour, William Sturt? In his *Saunters through Kent,* published in 1924, Charles Igglesden, says 'Sturt naturally became a great hero.' The author goes on to say that Sturt was fully compensated for his expenditure on arms for the battle, and that men from every station in life manned the barricades with him in the battle.

Another writer, J Sprange, in his 1780 *Tunbridge Wells Guide,* tells us that 'Mr Sturt, the Militia General, gained...the esteem of all his townsmen, with whom he has dwelt ever since, and by them is justly revered.' Sprang goes on to say that Sturt was 'some years since' master of the workhouse and that perhaps 'no workhouse in the kingdom is better regulated.'

In the *Gentleman's Magazine,* for September 1785, a journalist known only as 'S' (whom Browning suggests might be J. Sprange) also gives a brief account of the battle and praises Sturt's handling of it. 'He armed his troops as well as he was able, and disposed of them in a manner that would do honour to a veteran. He had a body to meet the enemy in front and he had a corps in ambuscade to attack them in the rear. He routed the assailants whose leader afterwards died in goal: he himself is still alive and has a soldier-like regard to the strong beer of Old England...'

Despite such praise for Sturt, the facts following the battle show that he was only briefly in charge of the militia. Barely three months after the battle, by July 28, 1747, leadership of the militia had been taken over by the Standing brothers. And when later, rewards are claimed for the defeat of Kingsmill and Woollet, the beneficiaries are a Stephen White and 13 others. Why is Sturt not even given a mention?

Browning suggests that William Sturt may have gone to live in Cranbrook as the researcher found two references to Sturt in the accounts of the Overseers of the Poor. There are also several additional references to Sturt in the Cranbrook records (along with more versions of his name wrongly spelt).

But what more do we know of the origins and life of William Sturt? In the registers of St Mary's, William was baptised on August 24th, 1718, recorded as the 'base born son of Elizabeth Start'. The next relevant entry shows Sturt's marriage to Ann Beeching on March 4th, 1753. Their daughter, Elizabeth, was baptised on November 12th 1755, and - sadly - buried on September 19th, 1756. William Sturt's second daughter, Ann, was baptised on June 27th, 1760 (The entry gives the parents' names as William and Anne Start - such spelling errors are common in parish registers).

There appears to be no record of the death of Sturt's first wife, Anne, but on November 5th, 1763, William Sturt, married the widow, Elizabeth Dudley, in St Mary's Church, Goudhurst. Their first son, William, was baptised there on November 23rd, 1764.

Following a Vestry meeting on Sunday, March 27th, 1765, William Sturt was appointed Governor of the Goudhurst Workhouse, with Elizabeth as Governess. There is, however, one puzzling thing about this appointment. It has been generally thought that after the battle of Goudhurst, the villagers were anxious to reward Sturt for his gallantry. It is therefore surprising to learn that Sturt's salary in his new post was as little as a third that of his predecessors. Browning's comment here is that Sturt and his family enjoyed the facilities of the workhouse - such as they were - and were even able to set up a barber shop - thus ameliorating the terms of his appointment.

Vestry records don't show how long Sturt held the position as governor of the workhouse or whether his other two children, John, born August 15th, 1766, and Sarah, born October 24th, 1770, were brought up there. What we do know is that there was a vestry meeting on March 15th, 1779, 'to agree to the hire of Brickwalls House for the poor of the parish,' the house 'being in the occupation of Mr Mathew Pope and Mr William Sturt or their assignees.'

There are two further references to Sturt by local writers. In William Cooper's *Smuggling in Sussex,* 1858, the author states that 'General Sturt was for some time prior to his death master of the poorhouse of Cranbrook.' Sprang's 1780 *Guide to Tunbridge Wells,* states that Sturt was still holding his 'place' at the Goudhurst workhouse. William Sturt was buried in St Mary's churchyard on June 25th, 1797.

Following on from these records, Browning asserts that 'there is little evidence to support the claims that Sturt was held in high esteem, remained in Goudhurst immediately after the battle, was able to indulge his soldier-like regard to the strong beer of Old England, or even share a part of the reward money - if it was ever paid.'

It may not be as interesting as the legend...but then facts seldom are.

Champion on 2 Wheels and 4 - an Unchallenged Record

NORMAN JOHN SURTEES (1934-)

When the 18-year-old John Surtees bought his first car, a Jowett Jupiter, it wasn't to help chat up the birds (there was insufficient time for girls, he wrote later). The car was for carrying motorcycle parts back to his lodgings. It was the beginning of a love affair with wheels that was eventually to bring him seven world championships on motorcycles and six Grands Prix wins with cars.

Norman John Surtees was born on February 11th, 1934 at the home of his mother's sister in the small village of Tatsfield in Surrey, right on the Kent border. (He was later to set up his business, Team Surtees Ltd, in Edenbridge, in Kent). The young John left

John Surtees after winning the 500cc class at the famous Nurburg Ring, about 1960

school at 15 to work for his father, a motorcycle dealer and racer. But after a couple of years, it was decided that he should broaden his knowledge of engineering. He underwent a five-year apprenticeship at the Vincent HRD Company's motorcycle factory at Stevenage and it was during these years that he rose to the top in racing.

John began his career on motorcycles in 1949 riding a Vincent Grey Flash that he had developed himself. He had his first win in 1951 and by 1954 had won 50 out of 60 races entered. During these apprenticeship years, he made it a point of honour never to let his racing interfere with his work, even if this meant sleeping in the back of the van with his mother driving - returning from a distant race meeting.

After transferring to Norton, he became British champion in 1954 and 1955. In 1956, riding in his first world championship series for the MV Agusta team, he won the world 500cc title. With great skill and courage, he won six further world championships on Italian bikes. In 1959, his success was rewarded with the MBE.

At a sports lunch at the end of 1958, Surtees found himself at a table with Mike Hawthorn, celebrating Hawthorn's world championship on four wheels, and Vanwall boss, Tony Vandervell. After a discussion as to whether a champion on bikes could also win in cars, Vandervell offered Surtees a trial run in a Vanwall. John showed interest but did nothing about it.

In 1959, Surtees won more races on bikes, including the Junior and Senior TIs on the Isle of Man. In October, accepting an offer to try an Aston Martin at Goodwood, he was surprised to be offered a contract on the spot. He declined the offer but nevertheless felt drawn to car racing.

He bought a Formula 2 Cooper and was invited to drive in the Tyrrell Formula Junior Cooper-Austin at Goodwood. It was a sensational race, leaving nobody in any doubt as to his natural ability. He was granted a full licence by the International Automobile Federation. A fortnight later, he made his Formula 2 debut by finishing second to the Lotus of Innes Ireland at Oulton Park.

This brought car racing offers from Aston Martin and Vanwall but still Surtees resisted. In 1960 he won his third 350cc and fourth 500cc motorcycle world championship. He was in great demand but - while still continuing on two wheels - began fitting in drives with Colin Chapman's Formula-1 Lotus team. In 1961, he finally quit bike racing altogether.

Surtees notched up a number of non-championship car wins, including the Mallory Park 1,000 Guineas race. Finally, in 1963, he signed for Ferrari.

Surtees was exactly right for the team at the time. Ferrari needed John's relentless dedication and the ability to pursue technical perfection. He was rewarded with his first Formula 1 Grand Prix victory at Nurburgring. In 1964 Ferrari produced the 158 V8 engines, which propelled Surtees to further victories - in the German, Italian, and Mexican Grands Prix. He thus became the only man to win titles on two wheels and four - a feat that still remains unique.

Early in 1965, he formed his own company, Team Surtees Ltd, with its headquarters in Edenbridge, Kent.

In October, during practice for a race at Mossport, near Toronto in Canada, Surtees had what must be his closest brush with death. Here's how he described the accident in his autobiographical *John Surtees, World Champion*.

'I remember climbing into the car but recall nothing more until about four days later. It was later pieced together that, accelerating past the pits, heading towards the downhill right-hander, I lost a front wheel. The car ploughed into a barrier, somersaulted over it and landed on top of me.'

He was pinned under the wreckage and drenched with petrol - which, mercifully, failed to ignite. Surtees suffered leg, hip and back injuries. For a few days, it was touch and go whether the patient would survive. Dr McGoey, from the local hospital, said Surtees was lucky not to have suffered paralysis. He described his patient as: 'A stiff-upper-lip Englishman who is determined to make a rapid recovery'.

He was released from St Thomas's Hospital in London in January 1966 and immediately set about getting fit again. Enzo Ferrari had complete faith in Surtees but the Italian press wrote that he now lacked the strength to drive the latest 3-litre Grand Prix cars. John proved them wrong by completing a Grand Prix distance and breaking the lap record. He then went on to win a non-championship race.

After the Le Mans 24-hours race, a heated argument broke out between Surtees and the team manager. Surtees stormed out and joined another team, Cooper. And although he won the 1966 Mexican Grand Prix, John may have regretted that his temper got the better of him. Referring to his walkout, he later remarked: 'That was costly to Ferrari and costly to me. I believe we lost one or two world championships as a result'.

In 1967, he met the challenge of helping Honda to make a return to Grand Prix racing with the Honda V12. But he hadn't foreseen the difficulties of working in Japan. Development was painfully slow, the car big, heavy, and temperamental. Despite working night and day, success eluded the project and Honda finally called a halt.

For 1969, Surtees signed for BRM but this was not a success and was complicated when John developed medical problems, including viral pneumonia - a long-term consequence of his Canadian accident. Nevertheless, he embarked on his own Formula 1 project in 1970, producing a number of Cosworth V8-engined cars. But the modestly financed team encountered sponsorship problems and ceased competing at the end of 1978, when John was once again hospitalized.

The hospital experience wasn't all bad, however. John - who had been divorced from his first wife, Pat, some years before - struck up a warm friendship with Jane, the ward sister. One thing led to another and they eventually married and settled down in their beautiful country house near

Edenbridge. They live there with their three children - Edwina, Leonora, and Henry John.

Friends and colleagues speak of John as a man with one aim - to win. But they remember too, a man who wouldn't delegate, who would go over the minutia of any project, even if it meant working from eight in the morning until midnight. And they also talk of a likeable, friendly man, unsophisticated and with a winning smile. His talent was tremendous and if he didn't always succeed in all he did, perhaps he attempted too much. As a racer - on two wheels or four - he was simply the best.

How does he see his own life? How has it been for him? 'The main thing is that whatever I've done', he says, 'has been from the heart. I loved being involved, first building and riding motorcycles and then driving cars - but above all, it's been competing'.

That's what it's all been about. Competing - and winning!

He changed New France to Canada

JAMES WOLFE (1727-1759)

Just as Winston Churchill wrote that his whole life had readied him for the war with Hitler, so it could be said that James Wolfe's 35 years were a preparation for his battle for Quebec. And it is for this extraordinary daredevil victory that Wolfe will always be remembered.

James Wolfe spent the first 11 years of his life in the Kent village of Westerham, in the house that was then known as Spiers and is now the National Trust's *Quebec House*. His actual birth, on January 2nd, 1727, took place a short distance up the hill in Westerham Vicarage, where his mother was staying.

There was never any thought that James would pursue a career other than that of the Army. Children's games played with his younger brother, Edward, were always soldiers' games. Their father was Lieutenant Colonel (later Major-General) Edward Wolfe.

James Wolfe at the Battle of the Plains of Abraham

Early education for both boys was in the Westerham village school. Then, when James was 11, the family moved to Greenwich. In the 18th century, officers' commissions could be had at a very early age and James was only 13 when it was arranged that he should accompany his father on an expedition to Carthagena in the war with Spain. Much to James' distress, however, a serious sickness prevented him from going. He was never strong and illnesses of one kind or another were to dog him for the rest of his life.

Less than a year later, when the 14-year-old James was playing in his garden, a messenger brought him an officer's commission in the marines. There is no record of his service with the marines and shortly after his next birthday, he was allowed to become an ensign in the 12th Regiment of Foot. He had no more than a few weeks to wait before his unit was moved to the continent, to become part of the British expeditionary force. They were initially based in Ghent.

During a period of peace, he studied French, mathematics and military engineering. In the winter, he was joined by his brother, Edward, who had obtained a commission in the same regiment. James was promised the post of adjutant of his regiment, an important job for a lad of 15.

By spring the following year, the Army saw action against the French. Blunders occurred on both sides. The French, who had trapped the English soldiers in a valley, missed the opportunity of destroying them and were driven from the field. The battle was historically interesting as it was the last occasion that an English monarch - George II - personally led his troops into battle.

It was about this time that James heard that his brother had died of consumption. His mother wrote asking James to come home on leave, which he could have managed. But he was determined not to let private grief intrude on his professional duties. He wrote to his mother of Edward: 'he was an honest and good lad...and always discharged his duty with the cheerfulness becoming a good officer. He lived and died as a son of you two should, which I think is saying all I can...'

James did eventually get home but for only a short stay. The Jacobite rebellion, under the incompetent leadership of Prince Charles Edward, broke out in 1745. The 'Young Chevalier' made his vain attempt to regain the throne for the house of Stuart.

The King's son, the Duke of Cumberland, had been appointed commander of the English forces and he was so impressed with James' conduct that he promoted him to brigade major.

When the English army marched north in pursuit of the 'Young Pretender', Major Wolfe was made aide-de-camp to the Commander, General Hawley. At the battle of Culloden, the Scots fought bravely but were well and truly beaten by the fully trained English forces. Wolfe stayed in Scotland and by this time was so hardened to the mechanics of militarism that he saw no wrong in Cumberland's savage 'punishment' of the Highlanders.

There is, however, an often-repeated story. When a wounded Highlander glared at the conqueror instead of saluting, the Duke of

Cumberland ordered Wolfe to shoot the prisoner. Instead of carrying out the order, Wolfe replied 'My commission is at Your Royal Highness's disposal, but I cannot consent to become an executioner.'

The next ten years of Wolfe's career - from the age of 19 to 29 - found him in battles on the continent and on garrison duty in Scotland. His conduct was on the whole exemplary, and promotion followed promotion. His health remained frail and at one stage, it is recorded he had his teeth filled with lead, adding more poison to his wretched body.

He spent the winter of 1747-1748 on leave in London. James fell in love with Elizabeth Lawson, well placed socially but with little money. His parents were against the attachment and anyway the lady refused him. She died unmarried in March 1759. Wolfe accepted his rejection philosophically and wrote, 'it took away my stomach for two or three days.'

He was a keen sportsman, took plenty of exercise and enjoyed much reading. He was aware of the gaps in his formal education and while in Glasgow, took lessons in mathematics and Latin. In Paris, he added social graces to his military professionalism. He had ambitions to stay in France for a year or two to perfect his French. But as he was now a lieutenant-colonel, the Duke of Cumberland pointed out, not unreasonably, that an officer should not be away from his regiment for any considerable time.

But things were stirring abroad and the time had come for Wolfe to make an entry on the world stage. William Pitt - who had plans for British conquests all over the world - was appointed Secretary of State and among his many qualities was his supreme ability to choose men.

In 1757, a campaign against the French in Europe was a dismal failure. It was said that if Wolfe's strategy had been followed, the result would have been victory rather than defeat.

But now Pitt's ambitions lay further afield. He was the only man in the government to recognize the potential wealth of North America, where the French were already making strategic gains around the Great Lakes and down the rivers to New Orleans. The first target was Louisbourg, the French stronghold at the entrance to the estuary of the St Lawrence River and the key to France's Canadian empire.

Wolfe was made Brigadier-general and put in joint command with another Kentish man, Colonel Jeffrey Amherst. They were well paired. Amherst was steady, Wolfe was dashing.

Wolfe was a great believer in the combined power of the Army and the Navy. 'Whatever diminishes our naval force,' he said, 'tends to our ruin and destruction...'

After arriving in Louisbourg, the British ships poured broadside after broadside into the French vessels. And despite the intense fire of the French batteries, the English troops were able to capture one line of defence after another till at last the French were forced to surrender. Wolfe wrote home to report that 'our loss in this affair, notwithstanding the most violent fire from the shipping, does not amount to much above 400 men killed and wounded; that of the enemy at least three times as much. The garrison, to the number of about 2,000 men, are prisoners of war; they laid down their arms this morning, and we took possession of the town...'

The whole area, along with neighboring islands, was now in British hands. Wolfe became 'the hero of Louisbourg'.

His health was again poor and he returned to England to report to Pitt and to take home leave. He visited his mother in Bath, where he fell in love with a lady called Katharine Lowther. They eventually became engaged.

In the meantime, skirmishes continued in Canada. Forts were captured, lost, and recaptured. The eventual stakes were high but little could be gained until the British took what seemed the well nigh impregnable Quebec.

Pitt invited Wolfe to dinner and during that meeting, he recognized the greatness in the man. Wolfe, he saw, would be the instrument most likely to bring his daring plans into fruition. It was Pitt's ambition that the whole of France's great western empire should fall into British hands. To achieve such a high stake, Pitt needed a man who was cool, daring and resourceful. He must also have a touch of genius. In Pitt's eyes, there was only one man for the job. And that man was James Wolfe.

But not everyone had the same faith. Wolfe's promotion to Brigadier had only been temporary while in service in Canada during the siege of Louisbourg. Some of the older officers, resenting the rapid promotion of this brilliant, eccentric, successful young officer, told the King that they thought Wolfe to be mad. The King made his famous reply - 'Mad is he? Then I hope he will bite some of my other generals.'

In June 1759, Pitt provided the best ships and men available for the expedition to Quebec. The British Navy was then the strongest in the world and Wolfe was given nearly a quarter of it. There were 9,000 specially picked men with combined ship crews amounting to 15,000.

The shoals and currents of the St Lawrence were hazardous. An English sailor - with a combination of skill and bravado - volunteered to be the pilot. 'I'll show you,' he boasted, 'an Englishman can go where a Frenchie daren't show his nose.' Seeing the English success, the Governor of Quebec wrote home: 'The English have passed 60 ships of war where we dare not risk a vessel of 100 tons by night or day...'

But the odds were formidable. The river itself was broad and treacherous and the whole area was well defended, with miles of earthworks, behind which lay the French troops, both infantry and artillery. Away to the left rose high cliffs, seemingly unscalable. Time too was against them. The Canadian winter was due any time, when the mouth of the St Lawrence would be frozen over. Anyone but Wolfe might have reckoned the situation unwinable.

The French sent sailing fire-ships, loaded with explosives, down river towards the English ships. Several fire-ships merely reached the shore and tipped over on to their sides. Most of the others were towed to a safe anchorage by English sailors.

The Grenadiers made a sudden dash towards the French guns but were repulsed with the loss of 30 officers and over 400 men. The next day, Wolfe censured them for 'impetuous, irregular and unsoldier-like conduct.' Such incidents made Wolfe worry if the entire project wasn't in danger of failure. This concern was reinforced by a naval defeat higher up the river.

Wolfe put three plans to his generals but they rejected all of them. An alternative scheme suggested by the generals was considered but had to be put off because of bad weather.

Wolfe's health broke down again and the news carried around the force that their general was stricken with the fever. But, sick as he was, General Wolfe had concocted a master plan to capture Quebec. It was a wild, risky idea but so unexpected that it might just work. He himself called it 'desperate'. He instructed his physician to 'patch me up for the work in hand, and then nothing matters ...'

Secret plans were drawn up in the finest detail. Ships of the British navy sailed here and there, confusing the enemy as to where the main attack might take place. It was said that for a whole fortnight, Montcalm, the brilliant French leader, never took his boots off.

Wolfe silently sailed up river with some 3,000 men. His battle orders anticipated Trafalgar. 'The officers and men will remember', he said, 'what their country expects of them...The soldiers must be attentive and obedient to their officers and resolute in the execution of their duty.'

But Wolfe had no illusions as to the great risk they were taking. On the night before the attack, he summoned an old school-friend, commander of one of the ships. Wolfe gave him the miniature of Katharine Lowther and asked him to return it to her, if he didn't live to see the end of the battle.

At midnight, on September 12th, 1,600 men were shipped downstream in almost complete silence. Not a light showed in the moonless night, the oars were muffled and no sound was to be heard. Nobody from the French side saw them slide silently downstream. In the meantime, mock attacks were being made elsewhere, further confusing the French as they wrongly guessed where the main attack was to come from.

Wolfe's eccentric behaviour was often puzzling to those about him. As his boat slid through the water that night, those nearest to the general heard him softly giving a rendition of Gray's *Elegy in a Country Churchyard*. He whispered: 'gentlemen, I would rather have been author of that piece than beat the French tomorrow.'

Then, out of the silent darkness, a voice challenged them.

'Who goes there'?

Simon Frazer, an officer in one of the Highland regiments answered immediately in good French.

'France'.

'What regiment'?

'Of the Queen's. Then he added, still in French. 'Don't speak too loud, you'll bring the English down upon us'.

They stopped at Fuller's Cove. This had been Wolfe's secret: a narrow path, zigzagging up to the heights 200 feet above them. Slowly, inexorably, the Army moved upwards. There were few defendants. The local French leader was captured as he leapt from his tent bed. Within a few minutes of the last soldier reaching the top, the heights were in British hands. By nine o'clock, Wolfe's forces were lined up on top of the cliff as if on parade.

The French forces swept through the city onto the heights towards the British, firing as they went. The British stood silently, their rifles pointed ready for action. Each man was like a frozen statue. At last their general raised his famous cane and a volley shrieked into the French troops. Another volley followed. The French wavered, broke, and fell back, leaving hundreds dead.

Wolfe rushed forward at the head of the charge. The first bullet hit him in the wrist. Without stopping, he wrapped a handkerchief around it. Another struck him in the body. A third shot hit him fatally in the breast. He fell to the ground. A young officer picked him up and brought him to the rear of the fighting, where he laid him on a Grenadier's coat. The charge kept advancing.

A surgeon was called for but Wolfe murmured: ' Do not trouble. All is over with me.' An assistant surgeon arrived but could see immediately that nothing could be done. Wolfe momentarily came out of his unconsciousness. He heard one of the soldiers shouting, 'They run, they run'.

Wolf struggled to sit up. 'Who run'?

'The enemy, sir'.

Wolfe smiled faintly as he gave his last order for one of the generals to cut off the French retreat. Then he fell back. 'God be praised, I die content'. He died in the officer's arms.

It was another year before French power was finally defeated but it was Wolfe's capture of Quebec that ensured a full British victory and a British Canada.

Wolfe's body was brought home in HMS *Royal William,* and landed at Spithead on November 17th with full military honours. It was brought to Alfege, Greenwich, where it lay in state for three days before he was buried beside his father in the family vault.

Wolfe is commemorated by Quebec House and his statue on the Green at Westerham. The Quebec House collection contains pictures, prints, books and many other objects associated with this Kent hero whose courage triumphed over his ill health.

Kent's VCs

The Victoria Cross, introduced by Queen Victoria in 1856, is the highest award for conspicuous bravery in the presence of the enemy that the British armed forces can bestow upon its members. Those who achieve the VC are men and women of extraordinary valour, who, oblivious to personal safety, carried out acts of self-sacrifice or extreme devotion to duty that put them in a class of their own. They braved bullets and explosives and were oblivious to danger, cold and heat - to enable them to achieve a military objective or to save the lives of their comrades.

In this chapter are some of the bravest and most interesting Kent VCs, set out in date order. We look at their lives and learn something of their acts of bravery. The medals that they wear have inscribed two words: For Valour.

Magnificent Survivor

ARTHUR DRUMMOND BORTON, VC, DSO, CMG (1883-1933)

Arthur Drummond Borton

Arthur Drummond was the kind of Englishman who made sure that the sun never set on the British Empire. This extraordinary man was twice invalided out of the Army, broke his neck in two places while at the front, and then went on to win the Victoria Cross, the Distinguished Service Order and to be made a Companion of the Order of St Michael and St George, as well as picking up a handful of other medals.

Arthur Borton was born at Chevening in Kent, the son of Lieutenant Colonel A C Borton. Arthur was educated at Eton and the Royal Military College, Sandhurst. He joined the 60th King's Royal Rifle Corps and in 1902 saw action in South Africa, where he received the Queen's Medal with three clasps (denoting three campaigns). This was followed by service in Bermuda, Ireland and India. In 1903, he was invalided out of the Army for the first time, as unfit for general service.

The start of the First World War found him fruit farming in the United States. He immediately returned to Britain and joined up with a Kitchener battalion of the 60th Rifles. But finding that there was no prospect of action in the near future, he joined the Royal Flying Corps, where he was appointed to be an observer. In January 1915 he went to France with the No.3 Squadron. On March 5th, during a reconnaissance mission, the plane crashed: the pilot broke both legs and Borton broke his neck in two places. After this, he was once again pronounced unfit for further service.

But the small matter of a broken neck did little to stem Borton's appetite for action. In three months, he applied for an appointment with the Admiralty and sailed for the Dardanelles. He was given the rank of lieutenant-commander and placed in command of two squadrons of machine gunners. His squadron joined the landing of Sulva Bay and they remained in the front line until the evacuation of the peninsular. For his services there, Borton was awarded the DSO.

After being cleared by the Medical Board, which had previously invalided him, Borton was, in June 1916, appointed second-in-command of the 2/22nd Battalion, London Regiment. They were first sent to France, then made part of the 60th Division and transferred to the Salonika front which was continuously in the front line.

In May 1917, Borton was made Lieutenant-Colonel and wrote home excitedly. 'I have at last obtained my ambition to command my own battalion and am the proudest man on earth. My only fear is that I won't last, as my general health isn't good.'

The Division was transferred again, this time to Palestine. Borton and his men were in the thick of the action, especially during the Gaza-Beersheba operations at Tel-el-Sheria. Borton wrote: 'We took our hill and the men did far better than I ever dreamt they would. They got within 500 yards of the enemy and then lay for over two hours in the open under heavy fire waiting for the artillery to cut the wire, their casualties being about 15 per cent. The Brigadier then got a message to me to know whether we could go without the gaps being cut. It was the one thing I had been hoping for, as I felt that no wire was going to stop us. I'd got the flag with the Queen's badge on it in my pocket, and when the time arrived, I tied it to my walking stick and away we went. I'd never been so damn proud in my life. The flag was a surprise to the men and tickled them to death.

'We got in practically without loss. We cut the wire 25 yards behind our own barrage. This of course meant a few hits from our own guns but not a soul in the trenches dared show his head and the moment the guns lifted, we were on to them with bomb and bayonet and scuppered the whole garrison. Everyone is longing for the next whack. I thought I'd got over my longings in this direction by this time, but the men are so wonderful that it is impossible to feel frightened. I always have, up to the present, but no more!'

The following week, Borton won the VC. The official account runs as follows: 'Under most difficult conditions in darkness and in an unknown country, he deployed his battalion for attack. At dawn, he led the attacking companies against a strongly held position. When the leading waves were checked by withering machine-gun fire, Lieutenant-Colonel Borton showed an utter contempt of danger and moved freely up and down his lines under heavy fire.

'Reorganising his command, he led his men forward and captured the position. At a later stage of the fight, he led a party of volunteers against a battery of field guns in action at point blank range. His fearless leadership was an inspiring example to the whole brigade.'

Borton wrote: 'As the light grew better, I found we were in a devilish awkward fix. We were swept by machine-gun from both flanks, and behind their artillery put down a barrage on top of us; and if it were not for the fact that the light was still so bad, we should have been wiped out in a matter of minutes. It was impossible to say where we were and hopeless to go back. So to go forward was the only thing to do and we went.

'One of the men had a football; how it came there, goodness knows. Anyway we kicked off and rushed the first guns, dribbling the ball with us. I take it, the Turks thought us dangerous lunatics but we stopped for nothing, not even to shoot, and the bayonet had its day. For 3,000 yards, we swept up everything, finally capturing a field battery and its entire gun crews. The battery fired its last rounds at us, at 25 yards.'

The battalion next distinguished itself in the capture of Jerusalem. For these and other operations in 1918, Colonel Borton was awarded the CMG and the Order of the Nile.

After the Turkish armistice, he tried to get back to France but instead was sent to Murmansk in February 1919. On May 14th, he embarked for home and demobilisation. In the same month, he was awarded the Order of St Vladimir of Russia.

In 1914, Borton had married Lorna Lockhart. But the years of living dangerously must have taken their toll. For he died at Hintin, in Kent, on January 5th 1933, aged only 49.

'Courage Beyond Praise'

JOHN HENRY COUND BRUNT, VC, MC (1922-1944)

Capt. JHC Brunt, VC

As dawn broke over the Italian town of Faenza on December 9th 1944, Paddock Wood's John Brunt fingered his temporary Captain's markings and prayed for a miracle. His platoon could be seen dug in around a country house, facing the formidable German 90th Panzer Division. The enemy counter-attacked the British forward position in great strength with three Mark IV tanks and infantry. The house was destroyed and the whole area subjected to intense mortar fire. The British anti-tank defences were destroyed and two Sherman tanks knocked out. The situation became critical.

But Brunt was a long way from admitting defeat and rallied his remaining men. He moved everyone to an alternative position and continued to hold the enemy infantry, although outnumbered by at least three to one. Grabbing a Bren gun, the captain killed about 14 Germans by himself.

Brunt's wireless set had been destroyed by gunfire and a runner brought orders for his platoon to withdraw to some 200 yards to his left and rear. Brunt remained at his post to give his men covering fire. When his Bren ammunition was exhausted, he fired a Piat and a 2-inch mortar left by casualties. Then he too dashed over open ground to the new position. This aggressive defence had, however, caused the enemy to pause, enabling Captain Brunt to take a party back to their previous position and retrieve the wounded.

Later in the day, the enemy attacked again on two fronts. Captain Brunt grabbed a spare Bren gun and leapt on to one of his tanks. From here - standing or sitting - he directed the Tank Commander's fire, ignoring the bullets, which whistled past him. Then, seeing a group of the enemy approaching from the left, he jumped off the tank and stalked them with a Bren gun. He killed some and caused the rest to withdraw. The retreating Germans fled so quickly, they didn't even think about removing the bodies of their dead.

Captain Brunt was always in the thick of any fight, rallying his men and firing on any target he could see with any firearm he could pick up. The citation for his VC states that 'the magnificent action fought by this officer, his coolness, bravery, devotion to duty and complete disregard of his own personal safety, under the most intense and concentrated fire, was beyond praise. His personal example and individual action were responsible to a very great extent for the successful repulse of the fierce enemy counter-attacks.'

Sadly, John Brunt was killed the following day by mortar fire. It was December 10th 1944. One of his men recorded later that 'a shell greeted us and killed Captain Brunt. It was the only enemy fire for the whole day, and it had to kill the best officer and gentleman in the battalion.' Brunt's Colonel Commander wrote: 'we buried him in the field Divisional Cemetery the next day. He was one of the most popular officers of the Battalion one could have. In the field of battle, he was one of the most forceful and courageous of leaders.'

John Brunt was born on December 6th 1922, at Priest Weston, Shropshire but by his teens, the family had moved to Woodlands, Paddock Wood, in Kent. He attended Ellesmere College until 1941, when he volunteered for the army. After training with the Queens Own Royal West Kent Regiment, he joined the Sherwood Foresters on New Years Day, 1943.

Brunt saw action in a number of battles - in Tunisia, the Holy Land and Baghdad. He was wounded three times. In Italy, in an effort to crack the enemy's line, Brunt's platoon crossed and re-crossed the River Peccia so many times, it became known as 'Brunt's Brook.' Then, on December 15th 1943, in what was described as 'the darkest night', Brunt led a terrific onslaught which reduced the enemy position to utter confusion. For this he was awarded the Military Cross

After Brunt had won his posthumous VC, his home town of Paddock Wood honoured its heroic son. The brewers, Whitbread, changed the name of their local pub from the Kent Arms, to the John Brunt VC. And when the new church of St Andrews was consecrated on Friday June 17th 1955, one of the most important parts of the new building was the beautiful Victoria Cross window, in memory of John Brunt.

Paddock Wood locals have other memories of John: on the cricket pitch and - one of his last acts at home - helping with the hop harvest. Another writer, W Goddard, remembered John Brunt as a Public School boy: 'full of high spirits in life and sport.'

Some years ago a past colleague of Brunt, an E Andrews, wrote to the 'Old Codger' in the Daily Mirror. He was fulsome in his praise: 'John Brunt', he wrote, 'was the best officer I have ever met...if all were like John Brunt, the world would be a better place'. There was a local memorial service after Brunt's death. The Vicar paid great tribute to 'young John' as he was known throughout Paddock Wood.

There is a memorial to John Brunt at the Faenza War Cemetery in Italy, and in the Soldiers' Chapel of St George, Lincoln Cathedral.

✳   ✳   ✳

'The Bravest Act I Have Ever Seen'Winston Churchill

THOMAS 'PADDY' BYRNE, VC (1867-1944)

Private Thomas 'Paddy' Byrne, VC

It was during the famous Battle of Omdurman in the Sudan in 1898, at the height of the great charge of the 21st Lancers, that 'Canterbury man Paddy' Byrne became one of the VC immortals.

Lord Kitchener's personal messenger - the man who'd delivered the order to charge - was wounded and thrown from his horse. Private Paddy Byrne could see the man was defenceless and at the mercy of the attacking Dervishes (an Islamic sect, famous for their dancing, commonly called the 'whirling dervishes'). Paddy had been shot through the shoulder and could not use his sword arm; he had also lost his lance. Despite all this - and again severely wounded - he wheeled his horse round, raced to the rescue, left-handedly routed the Dervishes and brought the officer to safety. A slash on Paddy's back was deflected by his bandolier. This was the second time this heroic man had been surrounded by Dervishes and fought his way out.

Another man in that famous charge was a Lieutenant Winston Churchill, acting as a war correspondent. He was an eye-witness of Paddy's gallantry and in his dispatch, he wrote: 'It was the bravest act I ever saw performed.'

Paddy was born in Dublin and joined the 8th Hussars at the age of 20. After about a year, he had transferred to the 21st Lancers, in which he served for 23 years, 11 on foreign service. He went through the whole of the South African war and retired on a pension in 1910.

He had courage beyond the stage of recklessness. In the South African War, still with the 21st Lancers, he was soldier servant to Captain the Hon Raymond de Montmorency, who also won the VC at Omdurman. After Captain de Montmorency was shot dead while reconnoitring, Paddy swore he would bring his captain back dead or alive and had to be physically restrained to prevent him galloping off on his heroic but useless mission.

At the outbreak of the First World War, Paddy rejoined the army and served at the Cavalry Remount Depot at Canterbury and later in the

Garrison Police. After the war, he was a messenger at the Cavalry Pay and Records Office. He also attended King George V's garden party for VCs at Buckingham Palace. Always a keen gardener, he was a prolific prize-winner at the shows of the Canterbury Allotment Holders' Association. When he retired at 65, he had served the Crown for 46 years.

In 1942, Paddy had his leg broken by an Army despatch rider and suffered frail health ever since. In October of that year, Mrs Roosevelt, America's First Lady, visited Canterbury where she stopped and chatted with Paddy.

A prominent member of the British Legion, he marched with the Kent branch of the Legion in the annual parades to Canterbury Cathedral. Paddy Byrne died at the Canterbury Municipal Hospital in March 1944, aged 77.

Sandgate's First VC

WILLIAM REGINALD COTTER, VC, DCM (1882-1916)

When his right leg had been blown off at the knee and he had also been wounded in both arms, he made his way unaided for 50 yards to a crater, steadied his men who were holding it, controlled their fire, issued orders and altered the dispositions of his men to meet a fresh counter-attack by the enemy. For two hours, he held his position, and only allowed his wounds to be roughly dressed when the attack had quieted down.

William Reginald Cotter, VC

'He could not be moved back for 14 hours and during all this time had a cheery word for all who passed him. There is no doubt that his magnificent courage helped greatly to save a critical situation.'

This is the simple posthumous citation for William Reginald Cotter, aged 35, given in the Gazette for March 30 1916. He had died at Lillers, France, on March 14th. Added to this extraordinary bout of courage is the fact that the Acting Corporal had only one good eye - the other was glass.

William Cotter was born in Folkstone in March 1883. At the time of his death, the family home was at 2 Barton Cottages, Sandgate. He was the eldest of six sons, all of whom entered the Army or the Navy. Only one survived the war. At the age of five, William went to the Roman Catholic School in Guildhall Street. Upon leaving school, he worked for several local builders.

He had always displayed a spirit for adventure. At a young age, he disappeared from home. After several months, his worried parents were on the verge of advertising him as a missing person when young William turned up saying he had run away to sea and apologised for causing his parents so much worry.

It was then that he joined the local regiment, the Buffs, at the age of about 20 and was put on the reserves. At the outbreak of war, he was called up and went to Canterbury. From there, he was transferred to France. His letters home were full of good cheer and in the trenches he seemed the happiest of men. He was always among the first to go to the aid of the wounded and the dying. He distinguished himself in bayonet fighting and in the December before his death, was recommended for the

Distinguished Conduct Medal.

News of their son's death first reached the parents by way of a catholic priest. Writing from the trenches, the letter gave news of his last hours on earth. The young soldier had received Holy Communion, extreme unction, and the last blessing. His last words were those of a hero: 'goodbye, God bless you all.'

In the December of the year he died, William's parents travelled to Buckingham Palace to receive the posthumous VC from the King.

'Perhaps the Greatest Individual Achievement'

CLAUDE CONGREVE DOBSON, VC, DSO (1885-1940)

Claude Congreve Dobson, VC

That's what *The Times* called it - 'perhaps the greatest individual achievement of the youngest and smallest branch of the Navy - coastal motor boats'. It was also called 'the scooter raid' - in the Royal Navy's great tradition of raiding and scootering away. A small, fast-moving highly trained force penetrated an enemy stronghold, inflicted a major blow on a much larger opponent, then got clean away with minimum casualties.

In 1919, Britain was still officially at war with the Bolshevik revolutionary regime in Russia, although the political situation was by no means clear-cut. The brief to the Royal Navy had been to blockade the Russian naval base at Kronstadt on Kotlin Island, near St Petersburg. And there were two Bolshevik battleships, just waiting to be targeted. Until the previous month there had been a ban on offensive action. This had just been lifted.

It was decided to use Coastal Motor Boats (CMBs) - 55-feet long, capable of 35 knots and armed with Lewis guns and one or two 18-inch torpedoes. At 1 am on August 18th 1919, a flotilla of eight of these craft left Cowan's base at Bjorko Sound, 30 miles east of Kotlin Island, under Commander C C Dobson. Each boat was manned by two officers and an engine-room artificer. On each, there was also a Finnish smuggler with good local knowledge.

By 4 am, they had reached the north side of the island to coincide with a diversionary bombing attack by 12 RAF Sopwith Camels. The CMBs slipped past a row of forts, reputed to be heavily armed (in fact, at least two of the forts had only rifles and machine guns). Even when the small boats roared into the inner harbour at around 4.25 am, the fort guns were ineffective - it was thought this was because the forts feared they would hit each other!

The destroyer *Gavriil* was one of their first targets but the torpedoes ran into the shallows and missed. With the help of searchlights from the forts, the Gavriil managed to sink three of the British craft.

Other British boats had better luck. One reached the inner harbour and successfully torpedoed the Russian battleship *Andrei Pervozvanni*.

Of the eight craft which entered the harbour, three were sunk and their commanding officers taken prisoner. In another, the captain was killed; his second in command, Lt Gordon Steele went on to sink two ships and gained the VC.

Commander Dobson (as he then was) was also awarded the VC 'for conspicuous gallantry, skill and devotion to duty: to the manner in which he organised, commanded and led the flotilla through the chain of forts to the entrance of the harbour, and to the work performed inside...subsequently returning through the heavy fire of the forts and batteries to the open sea.'

Claude Congreve Dobson was born on New Year's Day 1885, at Barton Regis, near Bristol, the youngest of the four sons of Nelson Congreve Dobson of Halifax, Nova Scotia. The young Dobson went to Clifton College and then to *HMS Britannia* in 1899, joining the fleet in 1901. He was promoted Lieutenant on March 30th 1906, having obtained 'firsts' in all his examinations. He gained experience in submarines then in big ships then back into submarines in the first part of the First World War. He was awarded the DSO for destroying a German U-boat off Fair Island.

In June 1918, Dobson was promoted to Commander and appointed to the Anti-Submarine Division at the Admiralty. Following his coastal motorboat service in the Baltic during 1919, he was in command of the flotilla at the base of this branch at Osea until it was closed. He afterwards went to Australia as commander of the Flinders Depot of the Commonwealth Navy and was promoted captain in December 1925.

Dobson retired voluntarily on New Year's Day 1935, on attaining the age of 50. He was promoted Rear-Admiral on the retired list the following year. He settled down in Walmer in Kent for the remainder of his life. He died in Chatham on June 26th 1940, at the age of 55, and was buried in the naval reservation of the Woodlands Cemetery in Gillingham.

The First Ranker VC

SIDNEY FRANK GODLEY (1889-1957)

At the school in Lewisham, Kent, where Sidney Godley was caretaker, the history teachers referred to him as Horatius, the ancient Roman who'd defended the bridge across the Tiber...'in the brave days of old.'

It was a good comparison. For that was how Sidney Frank Godley had won his VC - alone on a bridge with a single machinegun against the German hordes, in the First World War.

Sidney Frank Godley, VC

On January 3rd 1919, the *Bexleyheath Observer* published an interview with Private Godley, the week after he had arrived back home in Britain. Godley tells us, in his own words, how he won his VC - the first to be awarded to a private in the First World War. He also outlines his experiences as a Prisoner of War (POW). At this time he was living at 25 Butterfield Street, Lee, Lewisham, then situated in Kent.

Sidney Frank Godley was born in East Grinstead, Sussex, on August 14th, 1889, and attended the National School at Sidcup in Kent. He was a keen sportsman, excelling in football, cricket and swimming. He joined the Army in 1909 and was in the British Expeditionary Force to France early in the war.

On the evening of Saturday, August 23rd 1914, Godley was on the bridge over the Mons-Cond Canal in Mons, Belgium, at a place called Nemey. The Royal Fusiliers had suffered heavy casualties. 'We had taken up our positions at 5 pm ', Godley recalled, 'and heard the German guns. We shot at some of the advanced German cavalry. The rest of the night was quiet.'

On the following morning, Sunday the 24th, the Germans resumed shelling. Godley reports that one of the British gunners was wounded, then another. It was now about 9.45 am and Godley took over the machinegun, dodging through heavy German fire to do so. He had been there barely ten minutes when Lieutenant Dease, commander of the machinegun section, was wounded in the knee. He was hit a second time, in the stomach, then took about five rounds in the body and died. The lieutenant was also awarded the Victoria Cross - posthumously.

A general retreat was called and an officer asked Godley if he would hold on - to cover the withdrawal of everyone else. He readily agreed and alone faced what must have been two German divisions. He had no illusions about the position he was in. 'I made up my mind,' he said, 'I would fire as long as my ammunition lasted. I realised that there was not a possible chance of getting out of it. I would be either killed or taken prisoner.' When Godley finally did run out of ammunition, he took a hammer to the machine gun and threw the mangled remains into the canal. He made sure it was of no use to the enemy.

Godley made an attempt to get away but a shell burst behind him. He was blown off the bridge embankment on to the ground below. That was the last detail he could recall and woke up the following Wednesday in a German dressing station in Mons, wounded in the back and head.

As a prisoner of war, he was taken to Doberitz by train. He regarded the 'cruelty' of that journey as one of his worst experiences. There were 60 men, wounded and unwounded, all packed into a small railway cattle truck. Godley had no stretcher and had to lie on boards in the corner. In 96 hours, they were given two meals.

But, as luck would have it, matters improved soon after he arrived. He was in Doberitz Hospital until the end of the following January, during which time skin was successfully grafted on to his wounds. He was treated well, by skilled doctors.

Godley was transferred to Doberitz camp and was sent with a working party to lay a water main. The POWs were drenched to the skin and the following day refused to go to back to work without a dry change of clothes. However, they were forced out at the point of a bayonet - so each prisoner wore only a blanket.

At the end of a long day's work, they were each rewarded with one penny. A private threw it away in disgust. He was punished by being stripped of his clothes and forced to stand in the open meadow for two hours. The rest of the POW's were made to search for the thrown-away penny.

Godley was then put to work as a crane operator in a locomotive factory, where he said the sentries were the worst in Germany. On one occasion, the POWs were made to strip off their clothes in a public street in front of all passers by. At other times, men were punched and kicked for no apparent reason. Meals consisted of roasted bark brewed as coffee, black-greenish looking pudding 'quite unfit for Englishmen to eat,' cabbage water and a daily allowance of bread. They complained about the diet, after which - perhaps surprisingly - 'there was a great improvement'.

The POWs were released shortly after the armistice. Godley found conditions in Germany appalling. On the way home, he visited Denmark and felt 'we were back again among civilised people.'

Asked when he knew about his VC, Godley replied that he was informed by a British officer in hospital in 1914. He was decorated by King George V at Buckingham Palace, on February 15th 1919. The citation praised Godley for 'coolness and gallantry in firing his machine gun under a hot fire over two hours after he had been wounded at Mons on August 23rd.'

In April 1939 a bronze plaque in memory of the 4th Battalion, the Royal Fusiliers, was placed on the spot where Godley made his stand. Godley attended the ceremony together with the Colonel of the regiment, Major-General W. P.H. Hill, and 50 other members or former members of the regiment. However, in the Second World War, the bridge was destroyed. Fortunately, a Mons man rescued the plaque and hid it. It was unveiled on the new bridge in November 1961.

The citizens of Mons presented a medallion to Godley, who in turn bequeathed it to the regimental museum - the Royal Regiment of Fusiliers (City of London) Museum, Tower of London.

Godley died at Epping, Essex, on June 29th 1957, aged 68. The funeral service took place at Loughton, Essex, on July 5th. The pall-bearers were six fusiliers from the regimental depot and three volleys were fired over the coffin. Two buglers from the 1st Battalion sounded the Last Post and Reveille.

The Rev Edward Mellish, who had performed the ceremony at Godley's wedding to Ellen in 1919 (and won the VC himself while with the Royal Fusiliers) took part in the burial service.

In 1976, Bexley Council named a new housing estate as Frank Godley Court. It was a victory for Godley's nephew, Mr. P. H. D. Blazier, who had fought to have his uncle's name recognised in Sidcup. He said, 'my uncle was the first First World War ranker to get the VC. He lived in Sidcup and went to school in Sidcup and I have always felt his name should be perpetuated in some way in the town.'

Well, now it has.

* * *

The only Jewish VC in the Second World War

THOMAS WILLIAM GOULD (1914-2001)

Thomas Gould, VC

Early in the morning of February 17th 1942, two officers on HM Submarine *Thresher* heard a strange grating noise above their heads. They didn't know it then but this was to give the crew some of the most dangerous and tense hours they would ever experience. On the previous day, the submarine had sunk an enemy ship and survived a number of depth charges and an air attack of bombs and bullets.

They were lying off Crete, which had just been lost to the Germans, with the death or capture of some 12,000 British, Australian and New Zealand troops. It was a disastrous defeat and a great blow to Allied morale. The Royal Navy had seen three of its cruisers and six destroyers go down beneath the waves. Crete had little strategic value to the Allies but it gave Germany a base from which to bombard the Eastern Mediterranean - against Cyprus, Malta and even the Suez Canal.

But what could the noise be? As the *Thresher* began to roll, it came again - a loud 'clang' and a grating noise of metal rubbing against metal. The conning tower was opened and a dark object was reported to be rolling about on the deck. Could it be a bomb - 'from that blessed aircraft?' They knew it would have to be investigated personally and everyone in the immediate vicinity volunteered to go.

Leading Seaman Adams was first sent up to identify the object. He dropped onto the catwalk outside the conning tower and scrambled forward. On the side of the casing, just below the revolving gun was a large jagged hole.

This required closer examination by men who knew what to look for. Lieutenant O.D.W. Roberts, the first lieutenant, said he was the obvious choice. Kent man, Petty Officer Thomas William Gould was quick to say he would join him, and it was agreed.

It had been Gould's 28th birthday on the previous day. He was Jewish, a cheerful man, fond of boxing and swimming. His fair hair, blue eyes and good looks earned him the nickname of Brighteyes. Gould had had some five years on submarines. He was in charge of the seamen on the upper deck and knew well the layout of the submarine.

It was still dark outside and the use of a torch could give away their position. So they 'hooded' the torch and began searching. Soon their worst fears were confirmed. They found an unexploded bomb three to four feet long, five to six inches in diameter and weighing about 100 pounds. It was lying on the submarine's casing in front of a four-inch gun mounting. The tail fins were all but broken away so, as the submarine rolled, the bomb could very easily slip off the casing and fall on top of the saddle tank. The jar would probably be enough to set it off.

The officer in charge, Lieutenant Mackenzie, turned the submarine around so that the stern was against the swell. This was to stop the sub rolling. It was vital to remove the bomb as soon as possible.

It was cold outside. The water was icy. It took a few minutes for the men's eyes to get used to the dark. They realised that they could easily lift the bomb. But the position in which it was lying meant it would have to be man-handled along to the bow, about 100 feet away. Just then, the sub gave a lurch and the bomb rolled from the port side of the casing over to where a rail stopped it. It was difficult to get a good grip on the smooth surface, slippery with seawater. Carefully, they put the bomb into a sack and passed a rope around it.

The steel deck was also slippery with little foothold. About half way to the bow it sloped upwards. They cut away some of the casing. At last they were in a position above the sea. Was the bomb fitted with some hydrostatic device, which would be set off by contact? The two men couldn't be sure. They were finally in a position to carefully let it into the water. Mackenzie called from below, 'Tell me when you've got it to the stern and I'll send her full speed ahead.'

One of the two men called back. 'Steady now. I'll shout Now when we're about to ditch it.'

'There was a further brief pause. Then: 'Now!'

Down below, the sub's engines roared full speed ahead. The men gave a final heave and the bomb slid into the sea. Mercifully, there was no explosion. Everyone breathed a sigh of relief.

But the relief was premature. Shining their hooded torch, Gould and

Roberts discovered a second bomb inside the circular trunk supporting the gun. This was a far greater problem. It lay among a scramble of pipes and torpedo tubes. There was hardly room for a man. There was no alternative for the men but to try to wriggle along on their stomachs, through the hole that the bomb had made in the metal grating. They were now about as cramped as it was possible to be. They didn't recognise the type of bomb and jotted down the details.

It was now 2.45 am. Men on deck could, after a while, pick out their surroundings. But inside the casing, the blackness was absolute. Thresher was close to enemy territory and not far from where she'd carried out a successful attack the previous day. The enemy would sure to be out looking for them.

The two men were now in even greater danger. Any approach by the enemy would mean that the submarine would have to instantly crash-dive. Normally, a man left on deck would have some chance that he may be rescued. But Gould and Roberts were inside the casing. They were trapped. If the sub dived, they would hear the sudden roar of the air coming out of the ballast tanks before drowning.

Still working on their stomachs, on either end of the bomb, Gould pushed and Roberts pulled. The gap the bomb had made in the casing was not really large enough to exit that way so they aimed for a larger space some 20 feet away. Between them and this exit were a number of projections they would somehow have to get through.

The bomb suddenly made a loud twanging sound. Was it a broken spring trying to make contact? They braced themselves for whatever may come. But nothing happened. Nothing so far. But they couldn't reckon how long their luck would last.

Carefully, gently, they continued the pushing and pulling. Then another twang. Still nothing. Above them, a seaman peered down, relaying progress to the commanding officer below. Over half an hour went by. They were still a good 17 feet from the exit hole. The twanging continued. Push-pull. Push-pull.

This bomb had large tail fins; it was about three feet, six inches long and probably weighed twice as much as the previous one. They reckoned it to be about 200 pounds. And this time, it wasn't possible to wrap a rope round. They clasped the slippery surface with bare hands.

The two men moved slowly. Gould now had the bomb on his stomach while Roberts - going feet first - pulled Gould by the shoulders. In an interview given in the Herts Advertiser of April 18th, 1975, Gould described the two men's mission as 'like two rats carrying an egg.' Between them they made up a human sledge.

It was 45 minutes since the *Thresher* had surfaced. At last they were past the last obstacle. It was now possible for the seaman to give them a hand. Gently they rolled the bomb towards the stern. They gave the signal, dropped their lethal cargo over the side and the sub shot forward. There was only silence from the deep.

In June 1942, Petty Officer T W Gould and Lieutenant P S Roberts were awarded the Victoria Cross.

Tom Gould was the only Jew to win the VC in the Second World War. He was born at 6 Woolcomber Lane, Dover, on December 28th 1914. At the opening of the Granada Cinema in January 1930, he was the pageboy who presented a bouquet to the Mayoress. He joined the navy in May 1933 and served in the Far East for four years. He married Phyllis Eldridge in 1941 and they had one son. On January 13th 1945 Gould was made honorary Freeman of Dover. But at the time of his Investiture, he was living in St Albans.

In later years, Gould spoke of his VC as 'a mixed blessing - even as 'a millstone round my neck.' His wife said that after he was made redundant aged 48, 'nobody would give him a job because he was the holder of a VC. They thought he would take advantage of it.' In 1987, Tom Gould was so hard up he was forced to sell his house. He also did something else he swore he would never do: he sold his VC. It was auctioned at Sotheby's for £48,000, well over the estimate of around £25,000.

Nevertheless, there were many who said that this should never have been necessary - that it was very shabby treatment for a hero.

In his last years, Tom Gould lived in Peterborough, in Cambridgeshire. His wife, Phyllis died in 1985. Tom Gould himself died in December 2001 and is survived by the only son of their marriage.

Going Absolutely Ape

WILLIAM PHILIP SIDNEY, VC
(VISCOUNT DE L'ISLE) (1909-1991)

William Philip Sidney, Viscount De L'isle, VC

Some years after the end of World War II, a Guards' NCO visited Lord De L'isle's palatial Penshurst Place, in Kent and - with a twinkle in his eyes - volunteered to describe the act of valour that had earned De L'isle Britain's most coveted military medal. He was brief and to the point. 'The major,' the NCO said, 'went absolutely ape.' The comment was delivered with a wry smile but it was right to the point in describing an extraordinary act of bravery.

The official *London Gazette* of course put it more soberly. The citation begins: 'For superb courage and utter disregard of danger'. The action came during February 6th to 10th 1944. It was vital that the Allies should hold the Anzio Beach Head in Italy. The Germans attacked a British division and a continuous series of fierce local hand-to-hand battles were fought.

During the night of February 7th-8th, Major Sidney was commanding a support company of a battalion of the Grenadier Guards. When enemy infantry heavily attacked near his company headquarters, he collected the crew of a 3-inch mortar firing near-by and led an attack with Tommy guns and grenades, driving the enemy out of the gully.

He and a handful of men took up their positions on the edge of the gully to beat off the enemy again. However, some of the Germans reached a ditch only 20 yards in front, from which they could have outflanked the British position.

In full view and completely exposed, Sidney dashed forward to engage the enemy with his Tommy gun at point-blank range, driving them back, leaving a number of dead in his wake. Back again on the edge of the gully, he kept two guardsmen with him and sent the remainder back for more ammunition and grenades.

The Germans renewed their attack and a grenade bounced off Sidney's face and exploded. It wounded him and one guardsman and killed the second man. Single-handed and, although wounded in the thigh, the Major kept the enemy at bay until the ammunition party returned five minutes later. Then once more the Germans were pushed back.

Just as he was on his way to a nearby cave to have his wounds dressed, the enemy attacked again so he returned to his post and fought for another hour until the left of the battalion was consolidated and the enemy finally driven off.

The citation goes on to say that 'only then did Major Sidney, by that time weak from loss of blood and barely able to walk, allow his wounds to be attended to'.

Throughout the next day, enemy action was so close that it was impossible to evacuate Sidney until after dark. During all this time, although still extremely weak, he continued to be an inspiration to all with whom he came into contact.

There is do doubt that as a result of this action taken in the face of great odds, the battalion's position was re-established with vitally far reaching consequences on the battle as a whole.

Sidney was a man of many parts, befitting a descendent of the famous Elizabethan, Sir Philip Sidney - courtier, poet, soldier and statesman. (Family motto: whither the fates call me). Both men had the refuge of coming home to one of Kent's most famous houses, Penshurst Place, dating back 600 years. It was originally given to the family by the boy King Edward VI 'to his trustye and well beloved servant Sir William Sidney' in 1552.

His descendent, William Philip Sidney, was born in Chelsea on May 23rd 1909 and educated at Eton and Magdalene College, Cambridge. He was the 6th baron and a baronet, succeeding his father in 1945 and created a viscount in 1956.

He was commissioned in the supplementary reserve, Grenadier Guards, in 1929. After a variety of postings, he was promoted Major and posted to the 5th Battalion Grenadier Guards in North Africa as a Company Commander and was heavily involved in the Anzio landings in Italy, where of course he won his VC.

In June 1940, Sidney had married Jacqualine Corinno Yvonne

Voreker, the only daughter of Viscount Gort, VC, who was awarded the Victoria Cross in the First World War. It was therefore appropriate that after the Anzio battle, Sidney was decorated with a piece of Victoria Cross ribbon, cut from Lord Gort's tunic. Gort had flown in for the ceremony, from Malta, where he was governor. The two VCs stood side by side and took the salute as the guards marched past.

Sidney was presented with the Victoria Cross by the King at Buckingham Palace in October 1944.

In the same year, he was transferred to the regular Army reserve of officers for parliamentary duties and was returned unopposed as a National Conservative for Chelsea, his birthplace. He was appointed secretary to the Ministry of Pensions but was only in the Commons for a few months, before he succeeded to the Barony and took his place in the Lords. In 1948, he was appointed joint treasurer and in 1951, Winston Churchill made him Secretary of State for Air. He was the first minister to go up in a nightfighter, following this with a trip in a Canberra bomber; he even took flying lessons. But when Anthony Eden preferred a man from the Commons, Sidney was forced to resign.

In 1952, he made an 8,000-mile inspection tour of the Middle East RAF bases. On a visit to Australia, he visited the weapons research establishments at Salisbury and Woomera.

From 1961 to 1965, he was the last British Governor General of Australia. He was welcomed by the conservative Menzies government but opposed by the Labour opposition, who wanted an Australian in the post.

To broaden his connections with Australia, he bought two properties in northern New South Wales. He also found himself ahead of his time in his criticism of Australian architecture. 'In every city', he said, 'one sees the same dreary, glass-covered, elevated matchboxes, stacked up like a row of tombstones, their sky-lines decorated by fuel-oil tanks and lifts.'

His first wife died in 1962 and he married again in 1966 - to Margaret, Lady Glanosk, daughter of Major General Thomas Shoubridge and widow of the 3rd Lord Glanusk.

At the time of leaving the Air Ministry, he was made a viscount but abbreviated his title by deleting the 'and Dudley' at the end of it. He had once been a guest of the USAF HQ at Ruislip, Middlesex, as Lord De L'Isle and Dudley at the top table - to find that two places had been set for him!

He had friends all over the world and travelled widely until the end of his life. He never shied away from unpopular causes if he felt himself to be in the right. Despite his valiant efforts in defeating the enemy in the war, he raised a fund to brief an English counsel to defend a German accused of war crimes, Field Marshal von Manstein.

Lord De L'isle devoted himself to the maintenance and upkeep of Penshurst Place. In the year before he died, the family welcomed over 82,000 visitors. But despite the numbers, he never wished or expected to make money out of Penshurst Place.

There were to be no side-shows but he wasn't averse to making Penshurst Place more attractive to the children. There is an adventure playground, which was expanded and improved with some of the many trees blown down in the 1987 hurricane. There are medieval fishponds and the gardens are laid out in the same way as they have been for centuries.

Lord De L'Isle modernised the kitchen and other facilities and ran the Sunderland Room and the Endeavour Restaurant. Despite his early reservations about stately homes side shows, he did introduce two annual craft fairs and ballooning in the park.

But he also liked to keep Penshurst Place as a home. 'People who come here come to a house where a family still lives and in however small a way, share in the style of life enjoyed by the Sidneys over the centuries.'

He died in 1991, a few weeks before his 82nd Birthday.

BIBLIOGRAPHY

Refers to more than one hero

Abbot, P E, and Templin, J M A, *British Gallantry Awards*, Guinness Superlatives Seaby, London, 1971

Bisset, Ian, *The George Cross*, Frederick Muller, 1963

Bowyer, Chaz, *For Valour*, Grub Street Aviation, 1981

Buzzell, Nora, Compiler and Researcher, *Register of the Victoria Cross*, This England Books, 1988

Church, Richard, *Kent's Contribution*, Adams and Dart, 1972

Creagh, General Sir O'Moore and Humphris, H M, *The VC and DSO*, Vol 1, Standard Art Book Co, 1924, reprint by J B Hayward & Son, 1985

Crook, M J, *The Evolution of the Victoria Cross*, Midas Books, 1975, in association with the Ogilby Trusts

Dictionary of National Biography, various dates and editions

Flower, Sibylla Jane, *Debrett's The Stately Homes of Britain*, Webb & Bower, 1982

Imperial War Museum, *Illustrated History of the Victoria Cross and George Cross*, 1970

Johns, William Earl, *The Air VCs*, Hamilton, London, 1935

The London Gazette. Details of gallantry awards, various

Lucas-Phillips, C E, *Victoria Cross Battles of the Second World War*, Heinemann, 1973

Smyth, Sir John, *Great Stories of the Victoria Cross*, Barker, 1977

Smyth, John, *The Story of the George Cross*, Arthur Barker, 1968

Smyth, Sir John, *The Story of the Victoria Cross*, 1856-1963, Muller, 1963

Stannistreet, A, *'Gainst All Disaster*, Picton Publishing, Chippenham, 1986

Turner, John Frayn, *VCs of the Royal Navy*, White Lion Publishers, 1973

Victoria Cross Centenary Catalogue, Marlborough House 15 June-7 July 1956, 1965

Who's Who in Kent

Who was Who

Adams, William

Cooper, Michael, ed, *They Came to Japan*, University of California Press, 1965.

Hookham, Hilda, *Elizabethan Pioneer in Japan, The Times*, November 13, 1965

Makino, Tadashi, *The Blue-eyed Samurai*

Massarella, Derek, *Will Adams and the First Englishman in Japan*, in *Japan Society Bulletin 95*, November 1981

Smith, Henry, *Reading James Clavell's Shogun*, in *History Today*, October 1981

Animal Heroes

The Animal World. Various issues.

The People's Dispensary for Sick Animals, *PDSA Dickin Medal, the Animal's VC*. Booklet

RSPCA, annual reports and other publications

St Hill Bourne, Dorothea, *They Also Serve,* [Dogs in War] Winchester Publications, 1947

Bligh, William

Dartford Reporter, November 16, 1962.

Humble, Richard, *Captain Bligh,* Barker, 1976

Kennedy, Gavin, *Bligh,* Duckworth, 1978

Letts, John, *Best Stick to the Book,* in *Daily Telegraph,* February 17, 1996

Spencer, Richard, *The Mutineers Who Escaped Bligh's Revenge,* in *Daily Telegraph,* February 7, 1996.

Bosshardt, Alfred

Brown, Gerald, *Long March Prisoner Dies,* in *Manchester Evening News,* November 10, 1993

Christian Herald, November 20, 1993.

Daily Telegraph, November 6, 1993

The Guardian, November 6, 1993.

South China Morning Post, November 13, 1993.

Watson, Jean, *Bosshardt, a Biography,* OMF International, Monarch, 1995

Brunt, John

Birkett, Peter, in *Sunday Telegraph,* November 16, 1997

Blake, R L V ffrench, *The 17th/21st Lancers,* Hamish Hamilton, 1968

Firm and Forester, May 1998

Housley, C, *British Gallantry Awards,* in *The Sherwood Forester*

The New Poacher, October 29, 1945

Walker, Jack C, *The Beginnings and Bygones of Old Paddock Wood,* published by the author, 1985

Campbell, Sir Malcolm

Campbell, Dorothy, *Malcolm Campbell, the Man as I Knew Him,* Hutchinson, 1951

Campbell, Malcolm, *My Thirty Years of Speed,* Hutchinson, London, 1935

Campbell, Malcolm, *Speed on Wheels,* Simpson Low, Marston & Co, 1949

Kentish Times, November 23, 1934

The Times, January 3, 1949, obit

Westward, Colin, *The Bluebird Man,* in *Kent Life,* March 1985

Cotter, W R, VC

Folkstone Herald and other local papers

Dobson, C C, Rear Admiral, VC

Chatham News, June 28, and July 5, 1940

The Times, June 27 and July 29, 1940

Winton, J, *The Victoria Cross at Sea,* Michael Joseph, 1978

Dowding, Lord

Albeno, Kathleen, *Lord Dowding, Hero and Humanitarian,* in *Kent Life,* September 1970

Collier, Basil, *Leader of the Few, the authorised biography of Air Chief Marshal, the Lord Dowding of Bentley Priory,* Jarrolds, London, 1957

Dowding, Lord, *Twelve Legions of Angels,* Jarrolds, 1946

Probert, Air Commodore Henry, *High Commanders of the Royal Air Force,* HMSO, London, 1991.

The Times, February 16, 1970, obit.

Wright, R, *Dowding and the Battle of Britain,* Macdonald, London, 1969

Duke, Neville

Dorman, G, *British Test Pilots,* Forbes Robertson, London, 1950

Duke, Neville, *Test Pilot,* Grub Street, 1997

Duke, Neville, *The War Diaries of Neville Duke,* Grub Street, 1995

Shores, Christopher, and Williams, Clive, *Aces High,* Grub Street, London, 1994

Wingspan, Pilot Profile: Neville Duke

Fairclough, née Robins, Josie

Kent Life

Fire fighting heroes

Dover Express, Dover fire, October 4, 1940. Also English, John, article on the great fire, April 1, 1977

Humphreys, Roy, *Dover at War 1939-45,* A Sutton, 1993

Furley, John

Ashford Extra, November 22, 1991. Plaque

Brown, Joan G, *Sir John Furley and the St John's Ambulance Movement,* in *Bygone Kent,* Vol 6, No 12

Clifford, Joan, *For the Service of Mankind,* Hale, 1971

Furley, Sir John, *In Peace and War,* Smith, Elder & Co, London, 1905

Kentish Express, October 5, 1872, January 7, 1899, May 4, 1985, August 27, 1987

Mackintosh, Ronnie Cole, *A Century of Service to Mankind,* London, Century Benham, 1986

The Times, September 29, 1919, obit

Godley, Frank

Bexleyheath Observer, January 3, 1919

Hither Green Newsreel

Sidcup Times, September 3, 1976

Gordon, Charles

Encyclopaedia Britanica

Ginger, Dawn, *General Charles Gordon, Generous Christian and Gallant Warrior,* in *Kent Life,* January 1983

Hutchinson, Lt-Col Graham Seton, *Gordon and the Gordon Boys,* in The Gordon Boys' School, 1944

Major, Alan, *Canterbury's General Gordon Tree,* in Bygone Kent, Vol 6, No 10

McLellan, Doreen E, library pamphlet, 1986

Pollock, John, *Gordon, the Man Behind the Legend,* Constable, 1993

Gordon, Percy Henry

Chatham, Rochester and Gillingham Observer, November 9, 1912

Gould, Thomas, VC

Dover Express, June 12, 1942

Herts Advertiser, March 7, 1975, April 18, 1975, October 30, 1987, November 6, 1987

Jameson, Rear-Admiral Sir William S, *Submariners VC,* P Davies, 1962

Roe, F Gordon, *The Bronze Cross,* P R Gawthorn, 1945

The Times, December 7, 2001, obit

Turner, John Frayn, *VCs of the Royal Navy,* 1956

Winton, John, *The Victoria Cross at Sea,* 1978

Guinness, Henry

Evangelicals Now, April 1996, obit

The Scotsman, February 21, 1996, obit

The Times, February 21, 1996, obit

Heslop, Richard

Heslop, Richard, *Xavier,* Hart-Davis, 1970

Hudson, Col D T

Sunday Times [South Africa] October 7, 1984

Sunday Tribune [South Africa] November 5, 1995

The Times, November 10, 1995, obit

Kinlan, Henry, GC

The Journalist, March 1941

Lifeboat Heroes

Biggs, Howard, *The Sound of Maroons,* T Dalton, 1977

Morin, Nea

Alpine Journal, Vol 82, 1977. Also Vol 83, 1978, Vol 92, 1987

Birkett, Bill, and Peascod, Bill, *Women Climbing: 200 Years of Achievement,* London, A & C Black, 1989

Morin, Nea, *A Woman's Reach,* Eyre & Spottiswade, 1968

Mummery, Albert Frederick

Clark, Ronald W, *Six Great Mountaineers,* 1956

Dover Express, February 22, 1907

Unsworth, Walt, *Encyclopaedia of Mountaineering,* Hodder and Stoughton, 1992

Unsworth, Walt, *Tiger in the Snow, the Life and Adventures of A F Mummery,* Gollancz, 1967

Noel, John

The Alpine Journal, Vol 95, 1990/91, obit

Butcher, Barbara, in *Kentish Express,* February 25, 1988. Also May 3, 1990

Daily Telegraph, March 13, 1989, obit

Geographical Journal, November 1989, Royal Geographic Society, obit

Noel, John, Baptist Lucius, *The Map and the Compass,* publication by the author, London, 1940

Noel, John Baptist Lucius, *Through Tibet to Everest,* Hodder & Stoughton, 1989

The Times, March 13, 1989. Obit

Unsworth, Walter, *Everest,* Allen Lane, 1981

Parker, John Lankester

Barnes, C H, *Shorts Aircraft Since 1900,* Putnam, Aero-Publishers, 1967

Penrose, Harold, *British Aviation, the Pioneer Years,* Aero-Publishers, 1967

Smith, Constance Babington, *Testing Time,* London, Cassell, 1961

Taylor, Michael J H, *Plane Makers for Shorts*

The Times, August 24, 1965, obit

Pearson, Daphne

Brooks, Robin, *Kent Airfields in the Battle of Britain*

Brooks, Robin, *A WAAF at Detling, 40 Years Ago, Bygone Kent,* Vol 2, No 2, February 1981

Daily Telegraph, July 26, 2000, obit

Kent Messenger, July 27, 1940, also August 3, 1940

Brooks, Robin, *Kent's Own,* Meresborough, 1982

Police Heroes

Dover Express, July 15, 1927, an account of the gallant rescue by constable PC Pollington.

Ingleton, Roy, *The Gentlemen at War, Policing Britain,* 1939-45, Cranborne Publications, 1994

Kent Evening Post, May 16, 1991, article on PC Peter Farrell

Ogley, Bob, *Kent at War,* Froglets Publishers, 1994

Ryder, Sue

Dennis, Emily, in the *Bury Free Press,* November 10, 2000

Haymon, Sylvia, *We the Survivors,* in *The Times,* November 8, 1965

Kent Messenger, August 1, 1975

Morrow, Ann, in *Daily Telegraph,* June 21, 1978

Ryder, Sue, *Child of My Love, An Autobiography,* The Harvill Press, London, 1997

The Times, November 3, 2000, obit

Sidney, William Philip, Viscount De L'isle, VC

Chapman, Frank, *Kent & Sussex Courier,* April 12, 1991

The Times, April 8, 1991, obit

Sidney, Sir Philip

Howell, Roger, *Sir Philip Sidney, the Shepherd Knight,* Hutchinson, London, 1968

Steward, Alan, *Philip Sidney, a Double Life,* Chatto & Windus, 2000

Stephens, Rebecca

Stephens, Rebecca, *On Top of the World,* Macmillan, 1994

Sturt, William

Bygone Kent, various issues

Goudhurst Coronation Book

Surtees, John

Cooper Evans, Michael, *John Surtees, Six Days in August,* Pelham Books, 1968

Hamilton, Maurice, *Grand Prix-British Winners,* 1991

Henry, Alan, *Formula One Drivers,* 1992

Henry, Alan, ed, *John Surtees, World Champion,* Hazleton Publishing, 1991

Surtees, John, *Speed, John Surtees Own Story,* Arthur Baker, 1963

Taylor, Neville, in *Kent Life,* January 1992

Wolfe, James

Bradley, A G, *Wolfe,* Macmillan, 1903

Cumfrey, Amis, *James Wolfe - the Hero from Westerham,* in *Bygone Kent,* Vol 14, No 3, 1993

Garrett, Richard, *General Wolfe,* Barker, 1975

Grey, Adrain, *Heroes and Villains of Kent,* Countryside Books, 1989

Kent Life, April 1967, *Major General James Wolfe,* 1727-1759

Samuel, Sigmund, *The Seven Years War in Canada 1756-1763,* Lovat, Dickson & Thompson, 1934

Sevenoaks Chronicle, April 3, 1982. Photograph of the unveiling of the statue of General Wolfe at Westerham in January 1911.

Thomson, A A, *Great Men of Kent,* J Lane, 1955

Tomlinson, Norman, *A Strange Sickly Young Man,* in *Kent Life,* January 1976

Warner, Oliver, *With Wolfe to Quebec,* Collins, 1972

Wilson, B, *The Life and Letters of James Wolfe,* Heinemann, 1909

The Wolfe Society, 15-page account of Wolfe's life and work

INDEX

54; enters Paris in disguise, 54; Carlist War in Spain, 55; marriage, 56; Order of St John, 56; knighted by Queen, 56; war in Sough Africa, 56-57; Ashford Manufacturing, 57; death, 57.

47; awarded George Cross, 47.

Lifeboat Heroes, 81-86; beginnings of the RNLI, 81; Life-threatening rescue by **Peter Thomas, 82-85;** Thomas presented with RNLI bronze medal by the Duke of Kent, illus, 85; rewards for heroism, 82, 85; worst weather conditions, 83; why he does it, 85; in retirement, 86.

Maidstone, 67, 107.

Medway Fire Brigade, 48.

Mihailovic, Draza, Yugoslav Royalist, leader of the Chetniks, 77-80.

Morin, Nea Everilda, 87-91; on top of Harrison's Rocks, illus, 87; birth and early years, 87; family of agnostics, 87-88; first visit to Switzerland aged six, 88; first 'real mountains' at 16, 88; meets and marries Jean Morin, 88; Denise and Ian born, 88; graduating member of Ladies Alpine Club, 88; the first women-only rope, 89; first expedition to Himalayas, 90; still a climber at 70, 90; was it all worth it? 91.

Mouse, Lady de Mouse (dog hero), 16-17; illus, front cover and 16.

Mummery, Albert Frederick, 92-97; illus 92; birth and early years in Dover, 92-93; spine defect, 92; learning his craft on the chalk cliffs of Kent and Sussex, 93; blackballed from the Alpine Club,

93; assault on the Caucuses, 94; married in 1883, 93; birth of rock climbing in Britain, 94; a close shave, 95; death on the mountain, 96-97.

Noel, John Baptist Lucien, 98-101; disguised into forbidden Tibet 1913 and illus, 98; first glimpse of Everest, 98; his book *Through Tibet to Everest,* 98; two months AWL from Army; 99; First World War, 99; boyhood and early years, 99; commissioned into East Yorkshire Regiment, 99; official photographer to 1922 Everest expedition, 99-100; canonisation of St Bernadette and sole photographer, 100; death at 99 in Romney Marsh, 101.

OMF, 23, 26.

Paddock Wood, 153.

Parker, John Lankester, 102-104; illus, 102; joined Short Bros, 102; birth and early years, 102-103; polio, 103; making enough to live on, 103; very wide experience as test pilot, 104; Master of Guild of Air Pilots and Navigators, 104; death in 1965, 104.

Pearson, Daphne Joan Mary, GC, 105-107; illus, 105, 107; how she won the GC, 105-106; birth and early years, 107; early career as a photographer, 107; frequent illness, 107; emigrated to Australia, 107; death, 107.

Pegler, Julian, 111-113; Queen's

ABOUT THE AUTHOR

Bowen Pearse was born and brought up on his father's cattle station in Australia. After completing his education in Sydney, he was employed by a local advertising agency to write copy 'in the language the countryman understands.' He later travelled extensively in Europe and Asia and worked both as a copywriter and journalist in London, Hongkong and Tokyo. He lives in a 16th century Kentish farmhouse, surrounded by fields. This is his fourth book.

Bowen Pearse